D0266446

MAKING A
LOW-MAINTENANCE
GARDEN

MAKING A
LOW-MAINTENANCE
GARDEN

SUSAN BERRY & STEVE BRADLEY

COLLINS & BROWN

705853

MORAY COUNCIL
DEPARTMENT OF TECHNICAL
& LEISURE SERVICES
7\ 2 . 6

First published in Great Britain in 2000 by
Collins and Brown Limited
London House, Great Eastern Wharf, Parkgate Rd
London SW11 4NQ

Copyright © Collins & Brown Limited 2000
Text copyright © Susan Berry and Steve Bradley 2000
Illustrations copyright © Collins & Brown Limited 2000
Photography copyright © Collins & Brown Limited 2000

The right of Susan Berry and Steve Bradley to be identified as the authors of
this work has been asserted by them in accordance with the Copyright,
Designs and Patents Act, 1998.

All rights reserved. No part of this publication may be reproduced, stored in
a retrieval system, or transmitted in any form or by any means, electronic,
mechanical, photocopying, recording or otherwise, with the prior written
permission of the publisher.

ISBN: 1 85585 709 X

A Berry Book conceived, designed and edited by
Susan Berry for Collins & Brown Limited.

Editor: Amanda Lebentz
Designer: Roger Daniels
Editorial assistant: Loryn Birkholtz
Printed and bound by Dai Nippon, Hong Kong

CONTENTS

INTRODUCTION

There are numerous ways to tackle the issue of cutting down work in the garden, but if you want your garden to look attractive as well as be easy to look after, design is a key element that needs to be addressed at the outset.

IF YOU WANT a garden that looks after itself but which is not entirely concreted over, the first and most valuable lesson you must learn is to garden *with* nature, not against it. All growing plants make some demands, but these demands are reduced if the right plants are chosen for the conditions. You also need to abandon previously held notions about what constitutes a garden—that all gardens demand a central portion of grass with flower borders around it—and start to look at other alternatives. The options open to you are varied,

but the following features all contribute to a generally low-maintenance approach. First, an area where you can sit and relax that has some form of permanent, easy to maintain, hard surface. In a very low-maintenance approach in a small urban garden, the entire plot can be turned into a hard-surfaced patio, but in a larger garden it would be prohibitively expensive to pave the entire area, although gravel is an easy to maintain, less expensive option for larger gardens. Second, the planting can be much easier to look after if you plan it carefully.

LEFT Most of the surface area of a small city garden has been turned into a shallow pool, with a Japanese theme. Hard surfacing and water are good low-maintenance combinations, offering an attractive year-round design solution.

RIGHT Decking is one of the most versatile low-maintenance surfaces, as it will span different levels and heights, and is relatively easy to construct. It looks good in both urban and country settings.

LEFT AND RIGHT Natural planting, using self-seeding perennials such as foxgloves and poppies for a shady area (left) and candelabra primulas for a damp one (right) allows you to enjoy the benefits of interesting plants without the labour associated with formal flower beds, in which staking and weeding are a major chore. Although more work than hard surfacing or spreading ground cover, if you choose plants that are naturally well adapted for the conditions, it is a good option for gardens in which work needs to be cut down without necessarily being entirely cut out.

Evergreens are generally easier to look after than deciduous plants (less pruning, no sweeping up of leaves). Shrub borders and ground-covering perennials are the easiest options but it is vital that you choose plants that are appropriate for the climate and soil conditions, so that they thrive when left largely to their own devices. To this end, you also need to choose plants that are not too invasive or too fast-growing.

Third, it pays not to hanker after traditional flower borders that demand time and effort to look their best. New, but equally attractive and less time-consuming solutions involve planting perennials in drifts in a far more naturalistic way. However, this is still a time-consuming form of planting compared with, say, ground cover or evergreen shrub planting.

Fourth, water features are surprisingly low-maintenance and are a great visual asset in gardens in which hard surfaces predominate. Anyone opting for the hard surface solution would be well-advised to include a water feature to go with it, as the sound and movement of the water helps to counteract the rigidity of hard surfacing materials.

Fifth, you can turn a portion of your garden into either rough grass or semi-wild planting, which will not only benefit nature but ease the work in a larger garden. If you have only a very small area—such as a patio—you will need to find ways to make container planting less time-consuming by choosing plants that require less watering—one of the major time-consuming elements in any container-dominated garden. (See the chapters on easier surfaces and features, where choices are given a star (*) rating out of five.)

Finally, consider ways of dealing with essential garden tasks as effectively and efficiently as possible. Traditionally, one way of cutting down on maintenance was to blast weeds with chemicals, but this solution is not advocated here. Design solutions, such as mulches and ground covering plants, are a more natural and ecologically friendly way to solve the problem.

Your low-maintenance plans and solutions will depend on the size of your garden, your lifestyle, how much time you have, whether you have a small amount of time to spare regularly or time for periodic blitzes only, and also whether you simply want to reduce the labour involved in an existing garden or create a low-maintenance garden from scratch. Turning an existing labour-intensive garden into a low-maintenance one clearly takes some initial work (unless you hire someone to do the job for you), but once the job is done, you then save yourself a great deal of time and worry later on.

EASY SURFACES AND FEATURES

Gardens are much easier to maintain if a portion of them is devoted to hard surfacing, whether this is bricks, paving, decking or gravel. Choosing the appropriate surface for the setting is important, as is finding ways to combat the monotony of a single type of hard surface. This chapter looks at some of the options open to the low-maintenance gardener, and the levels of maintenance that the different solutions demand.

BRICKS AND PAVING

Slabs of hard surface, laid together in different patterns, are generally regarded as low-maintenance surfaces, par excellence. *The problem lies, however, in how to prevent large paved areas from looking very dull. The trick is to use complementary surfaces in different ways to create visual variety.*

RIGHT An attractive brick-paved alley in a shady entrance provides a hard-wearing, heavy-duty, low-maintenance surface.

THE KEY FACTOR in any laid hard surface is to ensure that it is properly laid on a well-tamped surface (which incorporates a solid layer of hardcore) onto which a layer of sand is then spread so that the slabs do not shift and distort the surface.

Whether you choose bricks or paving slabs is a matter of design choice and personal preference. York stone, for example, is singularly beautiful and durable but extremely expensive. Imitation stone slabs, if the colour and type are chosen carefully, can be very effective if your budget will not run to the real thing. Brick is priced somewhere between the two and is more time-consuming to lay, but looks as good as York stone in the right place. Interesting patterns can be created to add visual interest. All the above can be edged with other surfaces to create greater visual variety.

Once laid properly, you will have relatively few maintenance demands made on you, but the cracks between the paving stones can create weeding problems. It is best with paving slabs to make a virtue of necessity and to leave slightly wider gaps than normal. These are then filled with sharp sand and soil, and some creeping plants that do not mind being trodden on, such as thyme, the little erigeron daisy (*Erigeron karvinskianus*) or baby's tears (*Soleirolia soleirolii*) planted between the stones to form an attractive green carpet. In a large garden, you can let your hair down a bit and plant larger plants—*Alchemilla mollis* (lady's mantle) responds well to paving crack planting, and looks terrific, although you will have to not mind getting your legs wet in damp weather as you brush past.

LOW MAINTENANCE RATING ★★★★★

PLUS POINTS
+ Once laid, requires no maintenance
+ Useful for small areas near the house or for paths
+ Lasts indefinitely if properly laid

MINUS POINTS
− Expensive to lay
− Areas under deciduous trees will need sweeping in autumn

INTERPLANTING PAVING

If you bed the paving stones into a layer of sand rather than laying them on concrete, and space them slightly wider than usual, you can plant tough creeping ground cover into the cracks, which will make a weed-suppressing canopy.

1 Scrape out existing surface, and relay with sharp sand and soil mixture. Separate plants by dividing them into sections.

2 Plant with small plants at 15cm (6in) intervals.

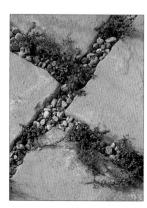

3 Surround new plants with a thin layer of pea gravel to reduce weeds while they are growing and spreading.

BELOW Paving stepping
stones set in gravel, and
interplanted with low-
growing carpeting plants,
make a varied, easy surface
to maintain.

ABOVE CENTRE Mixing
surfaces – here decking with
crazy paving – avoids
monotony without adding
to the work.

ABOVE Paving slabs can
inter-planted with Baby's
tears, for example, to make
paths more interesting.

DECKING

Wooden decks first found favour with gardeners on the North American west coast and in Scandinavia where timber is plentiful. They make an attractive, versatile, low-maintenance surface that is more durable than you might imagine, if laid with care.

WOODEN DECKING is ideal as a low-maintenance surface for patios and for gardens with changes of level, as the supporting structure can be easily jointed to span different levels. It is vital when creating a deck that you use properly treated wood for the sub-frame and ideally a durable hardwood for the deck boards themselves. Durable hardwood is the most expensive timber, but you can use treated softwoods successfully. Western red cedar is a good choice as it is naturally rot-resistant. The wood can be stained, ideally in soft colours such as sage green, dove gray or slate blue, that blend well with the planting.

The deck is usually laid with narrow gaps between the decking boards to allow air to circulate, and raised off the garden surface on brick piers, with heavy-duty, pre-treated wooden joists between the piers and the decking boards.

You can also buy the wood in carpet-tile like squares around 60cm (2ft) square that can be laid so that the timber strips they are composed of create interesting patterns. The latter are often a good solution for roof terraces, as they are fairly light, easy to lay, and require no nailing in place.

ABOVE RIGHT Decking makes a useful surface for uneven patios, as the joists can be manipulated to create an even surface without much effort or expense.

MAINTAINING DECKING

1 Once a year remove any deposits of green slime with a stiff wire brush.

2 Scrub the decking with water to which a little bleach has been added, which acts as an algaecide.

3 Softwood will additionally need an annual coat of preservative.

ABOVE Decking is ideal for roof terraces, as it is relatively lightweight and can be laid without puncturing any roofing membranes. If you live in a wet area, apply an algaecide once a year to prevent slippery surfaces.

RIGHT Mixing decking with railway sleepers and gravel adds visual interest without creating additional work.

LOW MAINTENANCE RATING ★★★★

PLUS POINTS

+ As a low-maintenance surface, decking is excellent. Requires only annual maintenance at most.
+ It is fairly durable – up to 10 years for a well-laid deck.
+ It is warm underfoot, looks attractive, and is relatively lightweight.
+ Ideal for surfacing roof terraces and balconies.
+ It is good for areas with changes of level, which would otherwise require extensive relevelling before being hard-surfaced.

MINUS POINTS

+ Does not last forever
+ Is relatively expensive

GRAVEL

By far the cheapest of all hard surfacing materials, gravel is attractive to look at, helps to reduce moisture loss, and allows a natural and relaxed style of planting in and around it.

THERE ARE THREE types of gravel generally used in gardens—pea gravel, river-washed pebbles or sandstone, which has a softer texture and more muted colours.

The Japanese have long used gravel, raked into patterns, as a design feature in their gardens. This looks laborious but in fact is not, provided the gravel is in an area where it is not walked upon. It will simply need to be raked over every few weeks—unless there are deciduous trees and shrubs that drop leaves onto it, in which case raking in fall will need to be more frequent. Gravel is not the most comfortable surface to walk on, so the best solution is to lay a stepping stone path through it. The steps can be of natural stone, concrete or wood, as preferred. Gravel can also be used in conjunction with railway sleepers to construct low-maintenance paths (see pages 22-23).

Before laying gravel, make sure the area has been cleared of perennial weeds, which should be burned. Once you have cleared the ground in this way,

you can lay a heavy-duty black plastic membrane (or old carpet) over the soil before laying the gravel, which acts as a weed suppressant. Failure to do this may cause problems, because although lack of light successfully prevents weeds from growing, the deterioration in the

BELOW By laying a gravel surface and positioning seating in a sunny corner of a large garden, you can create an attractive patio area quickly, easily, and with very little expense.

LOW MAINTENANCE RATING ★★★★

PLUS POINTS
+ Useful weed suppressor
+ Retains moisture
+ Allows you to plant through it easily
+ Cheap and easily available
+ Relatively easy to lay

MINUS POINTS
− Needs topping up occasionally
− Difficult to walk on
− Not ideal as a base for furniture

plastic and any thinning in the gravel layer will eventually permit the tougher ones to emerge through it. Promptly remove any subsequent weeds that do get a foothold before they penetrate the weed-suppressing membrane.

When laying gravel, you will need to provide a hardcore base and a retaining surround. Narrow wooden planks are the most economical choice for a surround, while tiles or bricks are particularly attractive. Usually, a layer of about 2.5cm (1in) of gravel is more than adequate, laid on a hardcore base approximately 5cm (2in) deep, so the whole area will need to be excavated to a depth of 7.5cm (3in). Larger pebbles can be used as a decorative surround to features, such as small splashing water features, or to create an interestingly varied surface texture—perhaps a row or two alongside a paved path, for example.

Gravel is the ideal material for small courtyard gardens with a formal design and principally evergreen foliage, which has the virtue that it sheds no leaves! Large architectural evergreens are ideal for this purpose: the hand-shaped leaves of *Fatsia japonica* or the neatly rounded mounds of *Skimmia japonica*. Walls can be clothed with evergreens, like ivies (*Hedera* sp.), *Schizophragma integrifolium* or *Hydrangea petiolaris*. Good-quality painted metal furniture suits this kind of setting. In a more rustic setting, a small gravelled area can be the ideal choice for a sitting area some distance from the house—possibly under a pergola clothed in climbers—and is relatively inexpensive to lay.

LEFT Gravel has been used for the entire surface area of this small courtyard-style garden in Australia. Natural log stepping stones provide an attractive path.

MIXED SURFACES

To avoid monotony over a large area, paving slabs, granite pavers, cobblestones, pebbles, decking and tiles can all be mixed and matched to provide an exciting, easy-to-care-for textural surface.

Any form of hard surfacing, no matter how intrinsically attractive the material, can look monotonous over a large area. One of the best solutions in a low-maintenance garden is to mix surface materials imaginatively to create interesting patterns and textures. You can do this in a variety of ways: first, you can use different surface materials for specific areas of the garden, such as bricking or paving for a seating area, with a gravel garden beyond. Or you could use decking close to the house with paving beyond.

Good-quality hardwood decking weathers to a particularly pleasing shade of gray, which marries well with paving and pebbles (for more about decking, see pages 14-15).

Consider the uses to which the surfaces will be put, and use them appropriately. Coarse thick gravel is not particularly easy to walk on, so use it for less frequented areas of the garden, or incorporate stepping stone paths to make thoroughfares across it.

LOW MAINTENANCE RATING ★★★★

PLUS POINTS
+ Needs virtually no maintenance once in place
+ Can be used to deal with awkard shapes and corners
+ Looks more attractive than a single material

MINUS POINTS
− Takes time to plan and lay
− Is relatively expensive

The main aim when mixing surface materials is to combine them sympathetically. Inexpensive concrete slabs can be made to look more attractive with surrounding areas of river washed pebbles set in concrete or paths could be given a narrow edging of gravel or pebbles. The occasional slab could be left out of the design and the space filled with smaller bricks or sets to create a randomly patterned effect. Equally, the spaces between the slabs can be wider than usual and filled with gravel or broken pieces of paving slab to make a more textural effect.

When mixing materials, choose colours that harmonize well and also fit in with the surrounding architecture. Use no more than three different materials, and contrast textures, perhaps, while keeping to a unifying colour way. Ensure that the hard surfaced area has a clearly defined edge, possibly finished off in a contrasting material. As with all hard surfaces, to last well they must be well constructed.

ABOVE This minimalist path and planted edging shows how hard and soft materials can be combined to create an almost sculptural effect that adds interest through changes of texture alone.

LEFT Wood, stone, and water combine to create a zen-like feel in a small garden. They make excellent companions and can be used together in a variety of ways, both formal and informal.

RIGHT Using infills of different materials will make larger areas of paving look more interesting, but will not add to the work once created. You could vary the size of the joints between the paving stones, or create an infill pattern with slates laid on edge and pebbles.

RAISED BEDS

If you are elderly or arthritic, bending over to tend plants can be extremely difficult. Even if you are not, it is much easier to garden when you're not constantly straining your back. Raised beds also provide perfect platforms for small plants that tend to get lost at ground level, as well as those with delicate perfumes.

APART FROM THEIR value in bringing the work in the garden closer to your own height, so that you do not have to bend, raised beds have other virtues. They bring small scented plants to a level where you can better enjoy their different perfumes and they can also be used to contain plants, such as mint, with a more invasive habit that might otherwise over-run a normal border.

Raised beds can be constructed from a range of materials including treated timber, brick and stone, but whatever material you opt for, remember to include drainage holes so that water can seep away naturally. The material used should be sympathetic to the planting nearby and to whatever materials have been used for the garden surfaces and surrounds. Any timber you use for a raised bed will not only need to be pre-

treated against rot, but the wooden frame will need to be lined with black plastic to extend its life. Former railway sleepers are ideal for raised beds, and they are heavy enough to need no nailing. A bed can be made simply by placing them on top of each other two or three high (they are, however, extremely heavy!) In areas where there is plenty of natural stone, raised beds can be made using a dry wall construction, in which no mortaring is required, and the stones are simply chosen to fit snugly on top of one other. Normally a raised bed would need to be at least 45cm (18in) high to grow fairly deep-rooted shrubs successfully, and at least 3ft (90cm) in height if you want to gain an appreciable difference in terms of having to bend less.

A raised bed can serve the same purpose as a large container, giving you

the chance to incorporate soil different to that in your garden and enabling you to grow a wider range of plants. An otherwise alkaline soil could have a couple of raised beds with acid soil, permitting rhododendrons, azaleas and pieris to be grown, which would otherwise fail to flourish. Higher beds are also good for raising cutting plants and herbs to a more accessible level, allowing an easier, back-saving harvest.

LOW MAINTENANCE RATING ★★★★

PLUS POINTS
+ Reduces back-breaking weeding
+ Easy to keep weed-free
+ Allows you to grow plants not naturally suited to the soil

MINUS POINTS
− Needs regular topping up with fertilizer
− Needs regular watering in dry spells

HOW TO CREATE RAISED BEDS

This bed is built on a levelled site on a hardcore base. It has an inner wall of cinder blocks and an outer wall of bricks. Using stakes and string, mark out the site of the bed, then calculate the width of the footing according to the width of the wall.

1 Concrete blocks are laid in place in the marked out trench and then left to set overnight.

2 Lay each corner of the outer wall. Set a string guideline between corners and infill with bricks.

3 Finish the wall with a course of coping bricks laid lengthwise across the inner and outer walls.

RIGHT Raised beds help to bring the planting up to waist height, making plants more accessible. In areas of natural stone, dry stone walling is a sympathetic construction material, but must be well-laid if it is to last.

TOP LEFT Unusual materials can also make attractive raised beds, as this collection of wooden posts shows.

PATHS AND STEPS

When planning a low-maintenance garden, paths and any changes of level are important considerations, since these are your major routes through the garden to carry out chores, as well as enjoy the view.

If a path serves an area that requires regular maintenance, it is vital that it is as direct as possible, although a gentle curve might well help prevent the design from looking too clinical. Much depends on the nature and style of the garden: in formally arranged gardens, straight paths are a key feature of the design. In a wooded area at the end of a large garden, however, the meandering nature of a path is half of the charm.

Path surfaces will be dictated by the style of the garden, too, but some are easier to maintain than others, and the last thing you want is a path that requires frequent weeding. Gravel is a good solution, with stone or log stepping stones to provide a solid base to walk on, but if you are likely to have to push a wheelbarrow over the path, you will need a firmer surface, such as paving or bricks. Paving stones set at slightly wider margins than usual, and interplanted with creeping plants, look good, and the planting will discourage weed growth if you use dense, carpeting plants. All paths should be laid on a solid hardcore base, such as gravel and sand, to prevent the paving material shifting.

Steps should be sufficiently wide and have treads shallow enough to be negotiated easily and safely. In large gardens, try to incorporate an alternative route via a sloping path for wheeled equipment. In smaller gardens, you will have to think through the planting carefully so that carrying heavy maintenance equipment is reduced to a minimum. Having gardened at a cottage on a terraced property, with a lawn on the top terrace, I am only too aware of the exhausting nature of carrying lawnmower and wheelbarrow up steps and, with hindsight, of the need to

BELOW In a gently sloping garden, wide, shallow gravelled steps, neatly edged with timber, make an easy to care for and attractive means of negotiating a minor change of level.

LOW MAINTENANCE RATING ★★★

PATHS
+ Must be wide enough for wheelbarrows
+ Must be well sited to allow fast and easy access to areas of the garden
+ Surface must be hardwearing to cope with frequent use

STEPS
+ Must have wide treads for easier use
+ Ramps must be provided for wheeled equipment if mown grass is part of the design

think about the maintenance issues of the design! Turning such a lawn to a more natural grassed area, with a twice-annual trimming, instead of weekly mowing, would have been a more successful solution.

In larger gardens, a more natural gradient with, for example, gravel and log steps is probably the best solution for dealing with changes of level, and it may well be worth the expense of hiring earth-moving equipment to make these one-time changes at the outset. A relatively small amount of initial planning and expense will certainly pay dividends in terms of ease of maintenance later.

LEFT In a woodland garden, natural log stepping stones, surrounded by bark mulch or ground cover, make a simple, appropriate, easy-to-care-for path.

ABOVE In this Japanese-style garden, a path has been given ornamental 'steps' using simple logs tied in place behind cut log uprights on a surface of gravel and mossy ground cover.

BOUNDARIES

All gardens need some form of containment—usually for security reasons if not for privacy. Although fences and walls require the least maintenance, there are some natural hedges that are relatively easy to care for.

To SOME EXTENT, your garden's boundaries are something of a fixture, particularly if you happen to have brick or stone walls. These are, in any event, pretty well maintenance-free and therefore a good choice for a low-maintenance garden, but the expense of building them is obviously far greater than erecting a wooden fence or planting a hedge.

Wooden fences will need to be looked after if they are to survive for a reasonable length of time, and the fencing posts must be of treated timber with a metal bracket to protect the ends from rotting, and with a spike to ensure it can be driven down easily. They also need to be spaced at intervals of 1.95m (6ft 4in) and driven at least 60cm (2ft) into the soil for a 1.2m (4ft) high fence, and 75cm (2ft 6in) for a 2m (6ft) fence.

Normally a wooden fence will need an annual coat of preservative, but this becomes difficult if you grow climbers against it—although the climbers will, to some degree, protect the fence from the elements and probably lengthen its life. You can grow climbers up a hinged trellis so that you can take down the trellis, complete with climbers, for the annual coat of preservative, or you can decide to let the fence cope as best it can and reckon on replacing it after a period of around 20-25 years.

RIGHT This fuchsia hedge makes a relatively easy-care screen, with the bonus of a wonderful flowering display in summer.

Hedges can be a major maintenance problem if they are already in place. If they are fast-growing shrubs that require regular clipping, your only solution is to grit your teeth, hire or buy good electric shears, and face the fact that you will have to trim the fence every six weeks or so in the growing season (April to September).

If you are planting a hedge from scratch, a mixed tapestry hedge is probably the easiest to maintain and is ideal for a large informal garden, but would look out of a place with a neat front garden. For more formal gardens, hornbeam is a good solution. Being deciduous, it makes a neat skeleton of bare branches and brown leaves in winter, but bursts into fresh bright

green growth in late spring. It will take slightly longer to establish than some of the fast-growing evergreens but then it will reward you by needing less frequent cutting. Its slightly hairy appearance between cuts looks a lot better than a privet hedge that is in need of attention.

For low formal hedges, box is a good choice because it is very slow-growing, thereby needing infrequent trimming, but because of its formal nature, the trimming must be done, although you can get away with doing it just two or three times during the growing season. Less formal hedges that require relatively less maintenance are lavender and santolina, which can be trimmed just once a year in fall.

LOW MAINTENANCE
RATING ★★★

HEDGES

+ Informal tapestry hedges are easy to maintain

+ Tough thorny shrubs, such as berberis or rugosa roses, make ideal informal hedges

− Formal, fast-growing hedges require a great deal of pruning to keep their shape

FENCES

+ Once treated with preservative, wooden fencing is virtually maintenance-free

− Must be properly constructed to avoid future maintenance problems

LEFT Dry stone walling is a maintenance-free boundary, provided it has been properly constructed in the first place. Drought-loving plants will thrive in its crevices. Tough weeds must be removed, but are easy to pull out.

BELOW LEFT Picket fencing and simple rough hewn timber make ideal fences in large country gardens.

BELOW For a country garden, a post and rope fence is ideal for marking a boundary. To make it secure, grow a tough, thorny shrub, such as berberis, on one side and underplant, as here, with ground cover.

LARGE WATER FEATURES

Once installed, a water feature requires relatively little maintenance and is therefore ideal for gardens large and small. A pond will also benefit local wildlife —particularly if you remember to make the pond edges accessible.

MOST WATER FEATURES are constructed from a heavy duty butyl liner, laid on a layer of sand to prevent sharp stones puncturing the membrane. The edges can be hidden with paving stones, pebbles or wooden decking, depending on the design of the surrounding area and the style of pond—a formal rectangle looks best with a neat edging, a more natural shape looks better with gently sloping edges in which pebbles provide a link between the rest of the garden and the pond.

To plant in a water feature to best effect, you need to create a couple of levels within the pond for plants that enjoy different depths of water: some like just their toes in the water, others like it ankle-deep and a few—such as water lilies—like to be fully submerged (and indeed need at least 1m/3ft of still water). Next to the pond, a small area of bog garden (a butyl liner with a few holes punctured in it so that the soil is damp but not waterlogged) gives you the opportunity to grow large-leaved plants that thrive in wet soil and creates a much more natural-looking bridge between the pond and the rest of the garden. Apart from a once-a-year or every-other-year division of the plants, there will be little else to do. If you stock the pond with fish, you will need to ensure that you have included enough oxygenating plants to keep the water fresh and you will need to feed them, but frogs and toads are maintenance-free!

RIGHT Almost the entire area of this deceptively large-looking suburban garden has been turned over to a shallow water feature, which is surprisingly easy to look after.

BELOW In this garden in Holland, where water is used extensively, the combination of decked surfaces and large pools makes a striking yet low-maintenance design.

LOW MAINTENANCE RATING ★★★★

PLUS POINTS
+ Very low-maintenance
+ Ecologically beneficial
+ Creates visual interest
+ Water-loving plants are singularly easy

MINUS POINTS
− Attracts mosquitoes
− Dangerous for small children
− Hard work to install

SMALL WATER FEATURES

Requiring minimal maintenance, small, unplanted moving water features bring an otherwise dull area of hard surfacing to life.

SMALL TRICKLING spouts, splashing millstones, pebble pools and wall fountains all give a garden extra vitality without adding to the workload once they are installed. The pump that recycles and drives the water will occasionally require servicing, but they otherwise need little attention. Small moving water features are ideal additions to a tiny town courtyard garden or patio, and can be situated in a corner or against a wall.

If you have opted for a large area of hard surfacing in your garden in order to cut down on the work, you will need to find ways to make this more attractive. Apart from mixing the materials (see pages 18-19), you can opt for some simple water features. You can choose a really simple, small submerged tank, such as an old sink for example, but if you want to get the best out of a small water feature, a pump that circulates the water, creating a small splashing fountain or a trickle from a spout, is worth purchasing. They are

not particularly difficult to install, but they do need a safe electrical supply with exterior heavy-duty leads and fittings, so employ a qualified electrician to sort out the wiring for you.

If you are pumping water through it, be sure to site your water feature where you get maximum benefit from the sight and the sound. A wall-mounted fountain trickling into a small pebble pool (which hides the pumping mechanism) is a good solution on the end wall of a small patio. The Japanese device of two bamboo poles, balanced on a central axis, so that the uppermost pole tilts and splashes out when filled with water (used traditionally as a deer scarer) is an attractive, and cheap, idea for any garden, but looks best in simple surroundings with foliage plants and hard surfacing materials. In a larger garden, a millstone with a trickle spout, surrounded by pebbles, could form the central feature of a large graveled area, for example. The water does not have to be deep and if you opt for one of the modern shallow pebble pools, you have both the benefit and sound of trickling water and the knowledge that it is safer for children. Be aware, though, that a very young child can drown in as little as 1in (3cm) of water, or less.

LOW MAINTENANCE RATING ★★★★

PLUS POINTS
+ Once installed, minimal maintenance
+ Annual service of pump only required
+ Bonus for wildlife of source of water
+ Pebble pools safer for children

MINUS POINTS
- Requires properly fitted electrical wiring for pump
- Not ideal for areas under trees, as leaves may foul water supply

RIGHT As well as looking pretty, this small pebble pool, with a wall-mounted fountain spouting water into it, makes a soothing sound as water trickles onto the pebbles.

ABOVE A raised pedestal with a spouting fish fountain (top) makes a marvelous feature for a formal garden; a Japanese-style bamboo water spout (centre) is an easy way to create splashing, moving water and a millstone, with a pebble surround (above), makes a safe, simple water feature for a natural garden.

PLANTING FEATURES FOR EASY UPKEEP

There are many ways that plants can be used to create low-maintenance features. The choice depends on the style, size, and form of the garden. While larger gardens may well need an area of rough grass or underplanting for a woodland area, small gardens may need simpler shrub borders or containers with drought-resistant plants that require little time-consuming watering. This chapter offers a range of ideas for easy upkeep planting.

GROUND COVER

One of the most attractive, and least arduous, ways to plant a garden is to use spreading ground cover, which will quickly establish itself in colonies to cover the ground, suppressing weeds, and saving you a great deal of hard work.

THERE IS A host of good ground cover plants, but you first need to establish the conditions in which you are planting them. Most do best in shade, but some prefer moist conditions and others like it dry. The plants vary from those that form a very low-lying carpet of foliage to those that grow to be fairly tall, so it is imperative to choose plants that fit in with the general design of the garden.

In a shady area under trees, you could cover the ground with taller ground covering plants that enjoy drier soil (the tree canopy will effectively create a dry area), while an area around a patio or gravel garden could be planted with spreading, mat-forming plants with shallow rooting systems that prefer free-draining soil. In a large garden, on heavy clay, plants that like moist soil can be encouraged to roam freely over banks, for example.

To create ground cover can be a laborious business that involves a certain amount of weeding in the first year or so. Ideally, use plants that spread quickly. Evergreen plants with low, spreading habit cast shade on the soil surface and prevent most weed seeds from germinating, but any ground cover is only effective if you have first cleared the ground of all weeds.

The easiest solution for plants with a spreading leaf canopy is to plant into black plastic and cover the plastic with bark mulch to disguise it. The area will then require no weeding, and the plant canopy will eventually spread to cover the area. For plants that spread by running roots, black plastic is useless and you will have to spend time weeding until the plants are established. This means you are probably letting yourself in for one or two seasons of weeding, but you will then have years of maintenance-free garden to enjoy!

PLANTING GROUND COVER

First you need to turn over the soil and remove perennial weeds and any large stones. Apply fertilizer to the area, and lay down the sheets of black plastic, overlapping any joints. If planting large shrubs, mark out the planting areas first and dig the planting holes before laying the plastic. Use a a sharp stick to mark the planting holes.

1 Lay down black plastic and weight the edges with stones. Remove plants from containers and mark their positions.

2 Cut a cross in the plastic over the planting holes, and remove the soil. Insert the plants, backfill and water well.

3 Close up the black plastic and insert remaining plants in position. Then cover the surface of the plastic with mulch.

LEFT Shade-loving mauve *Viola cornuta* makes an attractive carpet of ground cover under a tree.

ABOVE *Anemone nemorosa*—a woodland native—flowers around the base of a tree in spring.

ABOVE Little woodland plants, like *Asperula odoratum* and *Polygonatum,* make a spreading carpet round the trunk of an old tree.

ABOVE Brilliant red *Crocosmia* 'Lucifer' beneath a snake bark maple, *Acer griseum.*

LOW MAINTENANCE RATING ★★★★

PLUS POINTS
+ Excellent once established
+ Requires virtually no attention provided right plants are chosen for setting
+ Inexpensive means to cover ground

MINUS POINTS
− Takes time to establish during which time will need maintenance

ORNAMENTAL GRASSES

Handsome clumps of feathery grasses are easy to look after and offer long-term visual interest. They can be planted among shrubs and perennials or in specially designated ornamental grass gardens.

Everyone is familiar with grasses—if only in the firmly controlled environment of a mown lawn—but gardeners have often been nervous of using them in their own gardens. However, not all grasses make rampant ground cover, and there is a good range of well-behaved ornamental grasses to choose from (see pages 126-127).

Among those gardeners who extol the virtues of grasses are those who enjoy their sculptural and textural qualities; one of their long-standing favourites is tufted hair grass (*Deschampsia caespitosa* 'Goldshleier', or 'Golden Veil'), which has arching green leaves and flower stems in midsummer with plumes of silver-green flowers that reach about 1.2m (4ft). It needs moisture-retaining soil and full sun. *Milium effusum* 'Aureum' is another attractive clump-forming, similarly sized, non-invasive grass with

TOP LEFT *Stipa gigantea*, with its brilliant golden brown flowerheads, makes a worthy feature plant. It grows well in containers, too.

ABOVE A bold combination of *Miscanthus sinensis* 'Gracillimus' and *Crocosmia* 'Solfaterre' makes a striking feature against an evergreen backdrop.

LEFT Mixed clump-forming ornamental grasses can be grown together to create a distinctive ground cover garden that offers wonderful autumn colour. Here, delicate grasses like *Miscanthus sinensis* and *Stipa arundinacea* contrast with the ribbon-like leaves of a purple cordyline.

LOW MAINTENANCE RATING ★★★

PLUS POINTS
+ Easy to grow
+ Pest and disease resistant
+ Many different forms for different conditions
+ Good all-round feature

MINUS POINTS
− Only clump-forming grasses can be used, others are too invasive
− Will need periodic division and splitting about once a year

are generally robust and sturdy. They offer interest right through the year, their fall seedheads being one of their most attractive features.

There are grasses for every kind of situation—sunny or shady, wet or dry, acid or alkaline. You simply need to choose the appropriate grass for the setting. As Piet Oudolf and Michael King say in their book, entitled *Gardening with Grasses*, 'by choosing appropriate grass for local conditions, we have available tough, easy, low-maintenance plants for the contemporary garden, their dependability level ensuring the achievement of predictable results. A quick tidy up in spring, cutting them down to ground, is all that is needed in the way of maintenance.'

Grasses are an excellent way to soften hard surfaces or line paths. Good subjects for this purpose are festucas, *Hakonechloa macra*, *Pennisetum*, and *Luzula sylvatica*.

Why not replace the lawn with ground-covering ornamental grasses (see also pages 36-37)? Lawn grass refuses to flourish under trees, but there are many ornamental grasses that will thrive well even in very dry soil. *Luzula sylvatica* is a good bet for dry shade. The sedges, however, are particularly suitable for damp areas, as are the rushes.

bright yellow foliage and tiny golden flowers, but does best in partial shade. A good all-purpose candidate is *Stipa gigantea,* which grows in most soils in sun, its wonderful golden-bronze flower heads reaching a stately 2m (6ft) in summer.

When planting grasses in a flower border, it pays to use repeating clusters of the same grass at intervals down the border, for maximum effect. *Calamagrostis* x *acutiflora* 'Stricta', with its brilliant orange-brown spires, is ideal for this kind of design feature. In large gardens, the prairie-style ornamental grass garden makes a

highly successful natural, easy-to-maintain environment. The great American garden designers, Wolfgang Oehme and James van Sweden, popularized grasses with their prairie-style planting in the 1970s, and have used the giant pampas grass, (*Cortaderia selloana*) to great effect in repeating groups in a very wide border. Recently, gardeners like Piet Oudolf in Holland have been experimenting with new styles of relaxed planting in which grasses feature prominently.

Grasses are ideal for the low-maintenance gardener, since they require no staking or supporting, and

EASY-CARE GRASS

While a standard lawn is too high-maintenance (it requires weekly cutting and a lot of feeding and watering), there are other solutions using grassed surfaces that can be employed by the low-maintenance gardener.

BELOW Grassed areas that are cut less often, and where weeds are allowed to flower, offer the charm and beauty of a traditional lawn, but take little maintenance.

Larger gardens would be monotonous and repetitive without some grassed areas, but the lower maintenance solution lies in the way the grass is treated and managed. You can easily turn one end of a formal grassed area into a low-maintenance meadow, with a path mowed through the long grass for access to further parts of the garden. This will cut down existing work by roughly half. The meadow grass will need cutting only twice a year—once in summer and once in late autumn—and can be planted with spring-flowering bulbs and late summer-flowering wild flowers. You will, of course, have to tolerate 'weeds', such as dandelions, daisies and buttercups, but not only is this easy to maintain, it also provides valuable food for wildlife.

Make sure any grassed areas occupy those parts of the garden in which the grasses will flourish. Heavy shade cast by densely foliaged trees is not one of them, but lightly dappled shade is fine. Grasses are also ideal for sloping areas of the garden, provided the gradient is not too steep for occasional mowing to take place. Generally, meadow flowers do best in poor soil. Although flowery meadows are extremely attractive, to create a successful one is not really a low-maintenance concept, since a great deal of effort needs to be put in at the outset to get the soil conditions right to encourage the less rampant meadow flowers to survive more easily.

LEFT A grassy meadow can have a path mown through for easy access, while the meadow areas only require cutting twice a year.

ABOVE Areas of low-maintenance planting can be cut out of grassed lawns to reduce the amount of work. Large ornamental grasses are ideal, and require little care.

In addition to letting a portion of the lawn develop into a long grassed area, you can also ensure that the more frequently cut part of the lawn is planted with tougher, more durable grasses, such as *Festuca* and *Agrostis*. Some grasses are adapted for hot, dry conditions (like *Cynodon dactylon*) and others for more shady ones (like *Stenotaphrum secundatum*).

LOW MAINTENANCE RATING ★★

PLUS POINTS
+ Relatively high in maintenance but much less so than traditional grass
+ Ecologically friendly to local wildlife
+ Practical and inexpensive for larger gardens

MINUS POINTS
− Requires more maintenance than ground cover
− Not suitable for very dry or shady areas

SHRUB BORDERS

Shrubs, such as low-growing hebes can be used horizontally as well as vertically to cover the ground. Spreading cotoneasters and junipers are equally good for shrubby, low-growing ground cover.

THE CLASSIC low-maintenance garden that springs to mind is one of architectural evergreen shrubs. Although evergreen shrubs are among the easiest plants to maintain, a garden composed solely of evergreens lacks variety of colour and texture. The inclusion of some deciduous shrubs offers an unexpected visual bonus in fall, when the leaves of many of them turn wonderful shades of gold, bronze and scarlet. However, the leaves will need sweeping up so their numbers should be limited to a few outstanding specimens.

Shrubs are generally easy to care for, and although flowering shrubs will obviously benefit from regular pruning to encourage a good display of flowers, this annual task is really about the only demand made upon the gardener. Since their branches expand over a large area, often with a wonderfully spreading canopy of foliage, they make good weed-suppressing cover, too.

It is important to choose a balanced collection of shrubs with contrasting foliage, otherwise they can look dense and uninviting, but a mixture of brilliant light green, more waxy deep green leaves, red and purple leaves, and variegated ones with splashes of silver, white or yellow, all help to relieve what might otherwise appear dark and gloomy. Mound-forming evergreen shrubs, like *Skimmia japonica* and *Viburnum davidii*, are particularly valuable in a low-maintenance

garden, as are the small Japanese evergreens like *Rhododendron yakushimanum*, since they provide interesting form with consummate ease. Smaller shrubs like the hebes and euonymus, with evergreen foliage and small leaves, can be used as a foil for shrubs with much larger, more architectural evergreen foliage, such as *Fatsia japonica* or *Mahonia* x *media* 'Charity'—both extremely easy to

TOP LEFT Mahonia and *Lonicera* 'Baggesen's Gold' make an exciting contrast of colour and texture.

RIGHT In peaty acid soil, rhododendrons grow easily, along with some woodland ferns. The variegated, deciduous cornus foliage on the right helps lift the scene.

LEFT Mixed shrubs and perennial borders in a gravel garden make for easy maintenance. The variegated euonymus on the right provides good colour.

BELOW Spreading, mound-forming shrubs like hebes and junipers offer interesting contrasts of foliage ground cover backed by taller shrubs and trees.

look after. *Mahonia* has the added bonus for those in the south of attractive, bright yellow, scented flower spires in winter, when the garden is often looking bleak.

The inclusion of a small tree in the border, such as a witch hazel, hawthorn or a small crab apple, will improve the general appearance, and give it a lift. Witch hazel also provides good autumn colour and attractive, perfumed winter flowers. The front part of the border can be filled with easy ground-covering plants, such as *Heuchera*, *Tellima* or *Tiarella*, for example. (Lists of ground-covering plants for both sun and shade are given on pages 122-5.)

To ensure that shrubs grow well and stay healthy, you need to create a suitably large planting hole for them, with plenty of organic matter and nutrients, and water well in the season after planting. A healthy shrub is much less work than a sickly one, so it pays to keep an eye on them, and ensure that they are not suffering from any of the mineral deficiencies to which they can be prone. Before planting, check the acidity of your soil, since some plants, in particular *Pieris* and rhododendrons, will not thrive in alkaline soil. If you live in a limestone area, you will only be able to grow these lime-haters in containers with an appropriate peaty soil.

LOW MAINTENANCE RATING ★★★

PLUS POINTS
+ Evergreens are easier than deciduous shrubs
+ Provides useful screens and windbreaks
+ Offers flower colour and foliage interest
+ Works well in most gardens if plants are chosen to suit conditions

MINUS POINTS
- Needs pruning once a year
- May need treatment for diseases and/or pests

COTTAGE GARDEN PLANTING

A cottage-style border is far less work than a traditional one of herbaceous perennials. Cramming plants in close together means that they support each other, avoiding the need for staking and weeding.

ONE OF THE bonuses of the crowded, relaxed nature of cottage-style planting is that self-sown plants appear randomly. Another virtue is that cottage planting is not colour themed—it relies instead on a glorious mixture of colours that has the added advantage that self-seeding plants do not clash or look out of place.

The original cottage gardens were a quasi-haphazard mixture of ornamental and edible plants, and although vegetables are rather more work than flowering plants, a few in your mixed planting will not be too arduous. Opt for bush tomatoes, perhaps, which cope well in good sun with little pinching out or, if closely planted, tying up—but they must be watered well. Runner beans grown up stakes are another good-value plant in the cottage garden, as is rhubarb (provided it has rich soil and enough water). You can, if you wish, create your cottage-style planting in gravel.

Small beds of colourful mixed perennials grown informally in gravel (see page 123) will give you pleasure without much work, since the gravel (if laid properly) acts as a mulch against weeds.

Old varieties of plants tend to be more resistant to pests and diseases, as indeed are species plants generally. The important lesson if you wish to create a relatively low-maintenance garden is to choose plants that thrive naturally in the conditions, since your goal is to spend minimal time watering and feeding. If you do not already know what kind of soil you have, test it to determine the acidity/alkalinity. A simple soil test kit will determine this for you. Then ensure that you choose plants that thrive in the conditions. Most cottage-style plantings require reasonably good sunlight, so do not attempt this style of planting in a very shady garden; go instead for shade-loving ground cover (see page 124).

Another bonus of cottage-style planting is that the varied mixture of flowers is of great benefit to the insect population and you will, therefore, be doing your bit for nature. Scented plants are one of the great joys of a cottage garden so choose, where you can, aromatic-leaved or fragrant flowering plants. This will more than make up for any absence of flower power.

PLANT CHOICE

ANNUALS & BIENNIALS
Althaea
Cornflower *(Centaurea cyanus);*
Matthiola incana
Nicotiana; Nigella
Poppy *(Papaver)*
PERENNIALS
Achillea millefolium
Artemisia
Argyranthemum
Crocosmia
Delphinium
Geranium
Helianthemum
Irises
Lupinus
Lychnis coronaria
Potentilla
Rosmarinus
CLIMBERS AND TRAILERS
Clematis viticella
Sweet peas *(Lathyrus odorata)* (annual)
Nasturtiums *(Tropaeolum majus)* (annual)

TOP LEFT Although annuals are time-consuming, a few can be grown without too much effort. Traditional hollyhocks are fun to include in a cottage garden scheme.

RIGHT A glorious mix of self-seeding annuals and biennials, including poppies, foxgloves, and love-in-a-mist, runs riot in front of established perennial plantings of achillea and liatris.

LOW MAINTENANCE RATING ★★★

PLUS POINTS
+ Allows you to grow a mixed variety of plants
+ Ecologically beneficial mixed planting
+ Good for small gardens

MINUS POINTS
- Requires more control than ground cover or shrub planting
- Needs some gardening expertise to work well

ABOVE Include a few handsome verticals, such as *Verbascum olympicum*, to give structure to a loose planting scheme.

ABOVE Low-growing sun-loving perennials and small, self-seeding annuals, such as Californian poppies, in small beds are not labour-intensive.

DRIFTS OF PERENNIALS

Large drifts of a single planting, or a simple combination of plants, make a highly effective weed suppressant, as well as a distinctive and beautiful design element.

LEFT The creamy plumes of *Aruncus dioicus*, an ideal plant for damp, shady areas.

RIGHT Huge drifts of *Ligularia dentata* 'Desdemona' and burnt orange *Helenium* 'Moerheim Beauty' make a hot-coloured combination.

For best effect, you can't beat tough perennials, with their tall habit, good foliage, and strong flower colours. Among some of the best candidates for this kind of planting are *Coreopsis tripteris* with its daisy-like yellow flowers that last throughout the summer. It does as well in part shade as it does in sun. *Inula magnifica* and *I. helenium* are similarly brightly coloured yellow daisy flowers. Heleniums are also large and stately, *H. autumnale* having rust-coloured slightly drooping flowerheads. *Echinacea purpurea,* with its pink-bronze flowers and distinctive cone-shaped centres, looks equally good in large drifts. Just as large, but grown as much for its foliage as its oat-like plumes of bronzy flowers, is *Macleaya. M. microcarpa* is rather more invasive than *M. cordata*, but the seedlings are easily removed.

Of the smaller perennials, *Sisyrinchium* makes attractive slightly soldierly ranks of sharp, narrow green leaves with small yellow flowers. It makes an excellent choice for a long ribbon-like drift beside a path, for example.

In damp, shady, moisture-retentive soil, astilbes and aruncus do well, both with fluffy seed heads rising above the handsome architectural foliage.

Perennials need very little attention once established, provided you have chosen plants that are appropriate for the situation—shade or sun, damp or dry— and that they are robust plants with sturdy stems that require no staking. You can, in fact, even use the latter if you 'crush plant', that is, pack the plants in more tightly than usual, which will afford support and prevent strong winds from breaking stems.

It is imperative that the soil be in good condition before you plant to ensure healthy growth. You also need to create a generously sized planting hole for each plant, so that the roots can spread out easily and quickly, thereby establishing a firm base. If you wish, you can create areas of tall, medium or smaller perennials, but keep the plants to roughly the same height within an area to give the planting unity of form.

LOW MAINTENANCE RATING ★★★

PLUS POINTS
+ Once established, easy to upkeep
+ Makes dramatic visual statement
+ In keeping with new natural planting ideas

MINUS POINTS
− Visually unappealing in winter
− Not ideal for small gardens

ABOVE The tall yellow spires of *Ligularia* 'The Rocket' and the daisy-like flowers of *Ligularia dentata* 'Desdemona'.

LEFT Combine clashing colours to create eye-catching drifts, as here with the rich orange and yellow mixture of *Crocosmia* 'Emily Mackenzie' with *Achillea millefolium*.

PLANTING IN GRAVEL

Gravel provides an excellent moisture-retaining, weed-suppressing mulch for plants as a simple planting solution for hot, dry climates. Why not include small flower beds in a sunny gravel garden?

ONE OF THE principal advantages of planting in gravel for the low-maintenance gardener is that it cuts down on watering, provided you pick plants that are naturally able to withstand drought. A growing number of gardeners are now opting for this solution not only to cut down on work, but in order to help save precious water —Beth Chatto is among the pioneers at her garden in Essex, England, as she gardens in an area with scant rainfall.

Clearly, perennial planting of any description is not the lowest maintenance choice, but if you enjoy perennials and are prepared to do a certain amount of dividing and dead-heading, plus feeding, then this is a viable option.

Gravel gardens have become increasingly popular as climate changes in recent years have forced people to consider different options in their gardens. Regardless of climate considerations, gravel is a useful weed-suppressing mulch. It has an attractive informal appearance that suits a country setting much better than hard surfacing—and it is also a great deal less expensive!

Plants that grow well in dry conditions are ideal for this purpose and these range from the small alpines that thrive in rocky surfaces at high altitudes—saxifrages, sedums, dianthus, gentians and so on—to the taller perennials, such as cosmos, large members of the daisy family. The most attractive plantings in gravel will include a range of plant shapes and forms so that tall verticals, like verbascum and kniphofias, make a contrast with the more wiry small-leaved forms of many of the dry-loving perennials, like lavenders, perovskia and heleniums.

In a small area, after clearing the ground and turning it over well, you can cover the surface with black plastic, cut holes for the planting, and then cover the surface with gravel, which should effectively suppress weeds. You will need to offer the plants adequate supplies of fertilizer in

ABOVE RIGHT A mix of perennials and annuals, including anthirrhinums, poppies, marigolds, and love-in-a-mist, flourish in a sunny gravel garden by the sea.

RIGHT Sun-loving perennials, such as sedums, geraniums and erigeron, provide ground cover among foliage plants.

LOW MAINTENANCE
RATING ★★★★

PLUS POINTS

+ Useful for conserving moisture
+ Good solution for hot, dry climates/areas
+ Ideal seaside solution

MINUS POINTS

- Gravel needs occasional topping up
- Not a good idea where deciduous trees overhang area

order to compensate for the lack of natural nutrients. In larger areas, you will have to give the surface of the gravel a once a year application of systemic weedkiller.

If you are making small island beds in the gravel, then aim to put the taller plants in the centre of the bed, grading the sizes downwards until you have the very small alpines at the front. It will help to give character and form to the planting if you include a small tree or large shrub as the centrepiece of one of the beds—broom is an obvious choice and offers the bonus of wonderful flowers (scented, too, if you opt for the pineapple broom, *Cytisus battandieri*).

Among other suitable plants for an island bed set in gravel might be a few large perennials, such as some of the thistles, the giant verbascum (*V. olympicun*), *Verbena bonariensis* and the big sprawling euphorbia (*E. characias wulfenii*). Smaller perennials might include dianthus, sedums, saxifrages, small forms of gypsophila and little rock roses.

LEFT Railway sleepers and gravel make an easy-care surface with small, creeping thymes and saxifrages bringing life to the area.

FERNS

Varied in texture, shape, and colour, ferns are extremely beautiful as well easy to maintain. They were so popular in their heyday that Victorian gardeners devoted whole borders to them.

F OR A SHADY alleyway, to cover a bank, or to surround a feature in low-light conditions, nothing will do the job better than a fern. They are elegant, distinctive, and very well suited to urban gardens.

(As a note to dog owners, they, along with many other plants, react badly to being urinated upon. They literally curl up and die. If you have a male dog, do not have ferns!)

It is important to pick the right fern for the place. Most like moist shade, with free-draining soil, a few thrive in boggy conditions, and a few others will cope with sun (see pages 126-7).

To create a small fern bed or border strip in which the ferns will grow well, rewarding you with luxuriant foliage, you need to plant them properly (see below) ensuring that they have free

drainage, humus, and a certain amount of moisture retention. A sheet of perforated black plastic will help retain moisture, a layer of pea gravel over the plastic and humus over the top of that should certainly do the trick for the majority of ferns.

You can persuade ferns to spread and cover the ground if you peg the fronds down on top of humus-rich soil. The spores on the undersides of the leaves (they look like small brown scales) will then germinate to create small plantlets which can be removed and replanted.

Although generally maintenance-free, ferns may after a while tend to rise out of the soil, and you will need to give them an annual top-dressing of soil to prevent the roots becoming exposed and drying out too much.

ESTABLISHING A FERN BED

Fern beds are enjoying newfound popularity and are the ideal choice for the long thin strip alongside a house, that is often difficult to plant because the conditions are too shady for most plants to survive. If you pick the shade-loving ferns, you will be able create an interesting care-free feature.

1 Give ferns a good start with plenty of organic matter. Ensure the crown sits above the soil to prevent rotting.

2 Ferns benefit from an annual top-dressing of plant food, as many originate from the rich soil of woodlands.

3 To propagate ferns, peg the leaf down in spring and keep moist. Small plantlets should grow from the spores.

TOP In a shady border, surrounded by ground-covering oxalis and polygonum, the delicate fronds of *Athyrium filix-femina* provide a dramatic backdrop for a little carved figure.

ABOVE Planted under trees, ferns mix with other woodland plants (Spanish bluebells and Welsh poppies) in a relaxed natural planting.

LEFT An unused well provides a home for large damp-loving ferns in a shady corner of a garden.

LOW MAINTENANCE RATING ★★★★★

PLUS POINTS
+ Once established, requires minimal maintenance
+ Useful plants for areas such as shade where few plants grow happily
+ Relatively pest- and disease-free
+ Self-propagating

MINUS POINTS
− Different ferns require different conditions. Research needed to ensure right fern chosen for right place

DROUGHT-RESISTANT CONTAINERS

Plants from regions with low rainfall are naturally adapted to survive without watering, so choose easy-care plants from these regions. Many of these plants have little, silvery-gray leaves, or large woolly ones, both of which preserve moisture.

I F YOU GARDEN on a balcony or roof garden, or a hard-surfaced patio, your planting is limited to containers. Their principal drawback from a low-maintenance point of view is their need for frequent watering so your best option is to grow drought-resistant plants in them. Fortunately, there is a wide range to choose from—plants from the Mediterranean region are ideal, but they are often slightly tender, so on an exposed site you need to provide some form of shelter for them. Most tend to be sun-lovers, too—a shadier site limits your choices and the plants themselves tend to be smaller flowered. However ivy (*Hedera* sp.) is one of the best survivors of drought and poor soil, and containers with different ivies can look extremely striking, particularly if hung up where the leaves can trail.

The form of the plant will give you a clue as to the conditions it likes: those with silver-gray or felted leaves are well-adapted to dry conditions,

TOP, LEFT & ABOVE
Architectural sempervivums; a handsome variegated agave among sempervivums and pelargoniums; and a small trough filled with alpines.

lavenders and verbascums among them. Equally good are those with tough small leaves like thymes and helianthemums. Of the bigger-leaved plants, fleshy-leaved types, with a waxy surface, like the agaves, cordylines, and yuccas that hail from drier regions of the world, are good drought-resisters.

The ubiquitous geraniums (pelargoniums) are among the best-loved drought-resistant plants, and will cope well with little care, surviving without much in the way of food or water. Apart from the well-known regal and zonal pelargoniums with their brilliant flowers in singing reds, pinks, and magentas, there are some very attractive varieties with scented leaves,

like *Pelargonium* 'L'Elegante' and 'Lady Plymouth'. Their flowers are much smaller and more delicate, but their aromatic foliage more than makes up for a lack of flower power.

Sedums and sempervivums, with their fleshy succulent leaves and spires of bright flowers, are also extremely easy to care for, and a grouped array of small containers filled with different forms of both these groups makes an attractive display for a small patio table, for example.

The big foliage succulents like agaves and the equally handsome cordylines and yuccas also demand very little attention, and create a year-round feature with relatively little effort.

LOW MAINTENANCE RATING ★★★★

PLUS POINTS
+ Minimal watering required
+ Generally fairly tough and disease-free
+ Ideal choices for hot, dry climates

MINUS POINTS
− Some are prone to damage by too much water
− Not all are hardy
− Regular feeding and deadheading required

PLANT CHOICE

Agapanthus
Agave
Cistus
Foeniculum
Lathyrus latifolius
Lychnis coronaria
Nerine
Papaver
Penstemon
Perovskia
Senecio
Verbascum
Yucca
SMALL PLANTS FOR DRY SUN
Artemisia (smaller forms)
Diascia
Geranium
Helianthemum
Iberis
Dwarf potentilla
Sedum
Sempervivum
Silene
Stachys
Thymus
PLANTS FOR DRY SHADE
Alchemilla
Brunnera
Hedera
Helleborus
Hosta
Lamium
Millium effusum 'Aureum'
  (grass)
Pulmonaria
Symphytum
Zauschneria

LEFT Geraniums, *Helichrysum petiolare*, and daisies make an easy-to-care-for, long-lasting mixture that survives very well with minimal watering.

EASY EDIBLE GARDENS

Although edible plants are not a truly low-maintenance option, most people would like to have just a few that they can enjoy fresh from the garden. There are various vegetables, fruits, and herbs that are easy and rewarding to grow.

BY VIRTUE OF the fact that you want vegetables and fruits to provide you with a decent crop, you normally need to spend a fair amount of time looking after the plants to do so. They need more watering and feeding than ornamental plants if the produce is to swell and grow. However, if you are prepared to be undemanding, you can grow some vegetables and fruits with relatively little effort. Much depends on the climate and conditions. If you have good summer sun and a reasonable rainfall in the growing season, a lot of the work is done for you. Equally, if you are prepared to spend a modest amount of time and effort in the autumn digging in good quality fertilizer, much of the feeding is already in place. Pests and diseases are a constant problem with vegetables, but again if you are prepared to accept losses, you do not have to fight a major battle. Most of the problems with pests and diseases come from growing modern, less resistant varieties in large quantities. The principles of the old-fashioned cottage garden or kitchen garden, with small squares or short rows of plants, well mixed in together, was as good a natural deterrent to pests and diseases as any. Often certain

TOP All that runner beans need is to be supported and grown in rich soil. Watering, however, is essential in the growing season.

LEFT An herb garden is relatively easy to look after and will flourish with minimum attention in a dry, sunny area of the garden.

LEFT Growing ornamental flowers in with the vegetables, in cottage garden style, and edging the borders with herbs or box, cuts down on weeding and adds to the visual appeal.

ABOVE In this garden, a former vegetable area has been turned into an easily maintained mixed planting of herbs, flowers, fruits and vegetables.

flowers mixed in with the rows afforded natural protection—the classic natural deterrent is French marigolds planted alongside or in between rows of beans.

There are various vegetables that are easy to grow (see page 139), but generally, most root crops are fairly undemanding—leeks get few diseases, potatoes cope with less than perfect conditions (although the yield may be quite small) and radishes grow quickly.

Runner beans look attractive but need well-fertilized soil and decent amounts of water otherwise the beans will be dry, hard and stringy. Lettuces germinate very quickly and, if you can keep slugs at bay (with pellets or slug traps), you can get a good crop. The oak-leaved varieties look pretty as bed edging. The easiest fruit to grow is bush fruit, particularly blackberries and raspberries, which need relatively little attention.

LOW MAINTENANCE RATING ★★

PLUS POINTS
+ Certain vegetables and herbs are relatively low-maintenance (see page 139)
+ Good garden practices will cut down work
+ Reduced yield expectations mean less work

MINUS POINTS
- No cropping plants are entirely maintenance-free
- Most require some work during their growing season

DESIGNS FOR EASY UPKEEP

There is no single solution to creating gardens that are easier to look after than the traditional grass and flower bed garden. Much depends on the size of the garden and your own needs and preferences. In this chapter, the ways in which you can transform an existing garden to cut down on the work are given in detail, along with a gallery of six very different solutions to creating easy-to-care-for gardens.

WHAT ARE
THE OPTIONS?

To consider how to change your garden to a more low-maintenance style, you need to understand the implications of the changes in work terms.

UNLESS YOU HAVE bought an entirely new house, you will have some kind of garden already in existence and, unless you are exceptionally lucky, the maintenance angle has probably not been particularly high on the list of priorities of the previous owner, who may well have left you with a highly labor-intensive garden that she or he has failed to keep up adequately. What do you do?

The solution is two-fold, but both elements are highly practical. The first, and perhaps the most important, is budget. With money to spare, you can hire a garden designer to create a low-maintenance garden for you, but with money in short supply, you will have to turn yourself into an instant (and expert) garden designer. This is not quite as difficult as you might suppose, since a low-maintenance garden is without doubt going to have to include a large area of hard surface (or its easy-upkeep planted equivalent).

Your first task is to take a long, hard look at the garden and decide, if it has a big area of grass, whether you are prepared to endure the once-weekly schedule of mowing that this entails. If not, what surface will you replace it with? The options are paving (flags or bricks), decking (wooden lumber laid on joists), or gravel. Paving and decking look good and last well (particularly paving) but neither are cheap options, although reconstituted stone is not as expensive as natural stone, which looks much nicer. Decking is also expensive if the wood you choose is good quality and durable. It is, however, an excellent surface for covering uneven ground. Gravel is the easiest option, it is not particularly expensive, and it also looks good.

LEFT A terrace has been converted into a low-maintenance one using gravel and paving. The plants have been grouped into a central formal feature, which is effective both in terms of design and work, since watering and clipping can be done in one small area.

TRANSFORMING AN EXISTING GARDEN

Gardens are rarely created on virgin sites. In creating a low-maintenance garden, you need to know what to leave and what to recreate. Much depends on your own needs and preferences, and the nature of the site. If you want to keep maintenance down, the key is to go with nature, rather than garden against it.

The large majority of gardeners have either a traditional urban plot (long and narrow) or a typical suburban plot (wider, shorter, and somewhat larger). Depending on where you garden, you may need to seek different solutions for a lower maintenance alternatives.

Hard surfaces and foliage plants, along with formal water features, are ideal ways to create easy to care for gardens in the city, but hard landscaping would seem out of place in the country (and is extremely expensive to lay over a larger area), where more natural planted solutions are a much better bet.

Having decided on the principal surface area, your next decision is what to do with the planting. Are you going to go for the lowest-level maintenance (planted ground cover and shrubs that need no pruning) or a higher level that involves some work but gives you the opportunity to have more colour in the garden?

If you choose the ground cover and shrub route, it is important that you create some visual interest in the garden by breaking up any areas of hard surface and slotting the planting into it in arranged groups, so that the garden does not resemble a prison yard. (See pages 58-59 for more ideas on redesigning your garden.)

ABOVE A shady garden, overshadowed by a central tree, has an informal hard surface, interlaced with creeping ground cover, so that it is both easy to keep and provides variety.

RIGHT A courtyard in a large garden has informal cottage-style perennial planting in an area of graveled hard surface. Although not as low-maintenance as the other two examples, it is still an easier to care for option than more formal flower beds.

If you have a typical town plot, it is likely to have a square of grass in the centre, and borders and a couple of trees around the edge. Not only is this not particularly exciting visually, it is hard to control and maintain. The grass needs constant cutting (and a lot of feeding) and the trees may cast shade that makes the grassy area difficult to keep looking good. If you have shady borders, but these are not occupied by shade-loving plants, in time the plants will become sickly and straggly, meaning that you will need to spend more money and time on replacing them.

The best solution for this type of garden is to create a garden with easy to care for hard surfaces, but with enough variety in surfacing material to prevent boredom setting in. Decking, paving laid on the cross with planting holes, and a large water feature all cut down work while looking good.

If you have the typical suburban squarish plot, you will probably be faced with the usual complement of large grassed area (fiendish to mow), skimpy and rather unattractive curving borders, a badly laid patio near the house, and an overgrown vegetable plot. Apart from the fact that this garden can take hours each week to maintain, it also lacks any kind of structure. A lack of vertical elements makes the garden visually unexciting and, since nothing catches the eye as a focal point, the gaze tends to travel instead to the least attractive areas of the garden, such as an unmaintained vegetable plot!

The best solution in this scenario is to lay gravel where the patio was (cheaper for a large expanse), turn the end part of the lawn into a wild meadow, and create a much smaller vegetable area in a neat formal design with brick paths. Use box hedging (slow-growing only, needs clipping

ABOVE A large pool in this mountainside garden reflects the larger lake beyond, its shores a natural bank of pebbles and gravel. Planted with rushes, it provides an architectural and very low-maintenance solution to a garden on a sloping site.

LEFT This terrace over a stream shows how adaptable wooden decking can be. Relatively easy to install and maintain, it looks at home in country and town settings.

limiting the plant growth beneath them and thereby reducing the opportunity for weeds to grow. In larger, more naturally inspired gardens, the concept of weeds, as such, is alien anyway. Weeds were invented by obsessive gardeners with a masterplan for the planting, and a small army of gardeners to maintain it. A low-maintenance approach involves a more weed-friendly approach.

In acid soil, rhododendrons are superbly low-maintenance, since their evergreen leaf canopy prevents much growing under them. However, they only like areas of high rainfall, which limits their suitability. In very dry areas, dry stony soil discourages weed growth, which is a blessing, but it also discourages much else besides. Your solution here is to go for splashes of colour from drought-tolerant plants, positioned in areas that attract attention.

Many middle to large gardens have expanses of grass, which are immensely time-consuming. Your solution in this instance is to turn a good section of it into meadow grass (flowery or not).

twice a year) to break up the garden into compartments and arches to give the garden height.

In a larger garden of half an acre or more, your low-maintenance choices are very different, because it is highly unlikely you could afford to lay half an acre of paving throughout the garden. Happily, however, you have some simpler options precisely because the garden is large. For a start you can plant trees, which cast shade, effectively

RIGHT Large-scale drifts of plants, like these big banks of *Petasites japonicus*, effectively suppress weeds in more substantial gardens.

SIMPLIFYING THE DESIGN

Once you have decided to create a more low-maintenance garden, you need to identify the areas in which work can be reduced and come up with a new plan for the garden. You also need to consider how best to tackle the necessary work.

YOUR FIRST STEP is to examine the garden carefully and work out which features you wish to keep and which you need to lose, if you are to cut work down to a minimum. The garden shown below right is typical of many small gardens, with a small patio, a large area of mown grass, and flower borders around the edges. Unfortunately, this very classical design is also highly labour-intensive. Not only does the lawn need mowing once a week during spring and summer, but the flower beds are unlikely to have been created with the work element in mind. They almost certainly contain perennials and annuals that have been chosen for their preferred flowering performance, rather than their ability to maintain themselves in a trouble-free manner. To create a more low-maintenance garden, you need to isolate and identify the most time-consuming elements, and then find alternatives to them.

TRANSFORMING A GARDEN

In the plan, below, the lawn area has been replaced by gravel, with a stepping stone path to the garden shed, and to a seat (where you will now have time to relax!). The planting has been much simplified to consist of fewer plants, with shrubs replacing some of the perennials (see pages 60-61). The patio area of the garden has been much extended, and made more visually interesting by laying the paving stones on the diagonal. When creating more hard surfaced area, it is important to find ways to alleviate its potential boring expanse by mixing surfaces. A water feature has also been added to create visual interest.

HIGH-MAINTENANCE GARDEN

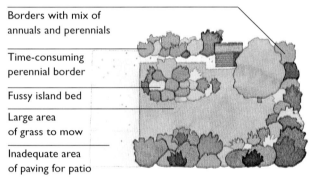

Borders with mix of annuals and perennials

Time-consuming perennial border

Fussy island bed

Large area of grass to mow

Inadequate area of paving for patio

NEW LOW-MAINTENANCE DESIGN

Arches provide support for easy-care climbers

Paved area for leisure

Raised pool— easier to maintain

Permanent shrubs—only annual pruning required

Stepping stone path in gravel— no weeding

Seat (also for relaxing!)

CREATING THE PLAN

You need to consider the best way to tackle the changes you intend to make. In the first instance, measure your garden and translate these measurements onto graph paper, so that you have a scale plan of the garden. (This also helps you determine costs of features such as as gravel and paving.) Map in the main areas of change—in this case, the new enlarged patio, the gravel replacement for the lawn—mark in any major features, such as trees that are staying, and the new pool. Then you need to draw in the major planting elements, in this case the position of shrubs replacing perennials. Finally, you can flesh out the plan with the smaller design features, such as the position of the bench and shed, the stepping stone path, and the pergola over it.

1 THE KEY DESIGN ELEMENTS

Map out your design on paper, drawing in major features, such as the area for the patio, the area to be gravelled and the area for planting, as well as any retained features (such as the shed and an existing tree).

2 THE MAJOR PLANTING ADDED

Start to flesh out the design by working out the direction of the path, the form of the planting that then follows this path, and the style of the planting.

3 ADDING THE DESIGN DETAILS

Finally, when the major construction elements have been finished, decide on the detailed elements: the pergola over the path, the raised pond next to the patio, and the positioning of the seat at the end of the path.

LOW-MAINTENANCE CHECKLIST

When considering your new low-maintenance design, check the following:
• Do your paths lead sensibly to important features, sheds, seats, etc?
• Have you considered the aspect when siting patio areas—in or out of sun, for example?
• Are your paths wide enough for wheelbarrows, if necessary?
• Will deciduous trees overhang patios or ponds, causing problems with fallen leaves?
• Have you left a secluded but accessible space for a tool shed?

STAGING THE WORK

It is unlikely that you will be able to carry out all the work in one go, so the next step is to consider how to go about it. You may find it best to stage the work, tackling one stage at a time (see Transforming a garden, pages 62-63). In this instance, the patio area near the house is enlarged in stage one, the mown area replaced with gravel in stage two, and the planting revised and adapted in stage three. The design details are then added when these major construction elements have been finished.

SIMPLIFYING BORDERS

Although beautiful, traditional style perennial flower borders are hard work. If you have inherited a flower border that is arduous to maintain, it might be worth replanting it to reduce the work by introducing a few shrubs and grasses among the perennial flowers.

FOR MANY PEOPLE, a garden is not much to write home about unless it has attractive borders. The ground cover that makes a garden so easy to maintain does not always appeal to those who like flower colour and variety. If you belong to this latter group, but still want to reduce the load in the garden, then consider planting or replanting your border or borders in a less labour-intensive way.

Try to reduce the numbers of plants and go for ones with form and texture as well as colour. Look for attractive foliage as well as flowers, and try to ensure that you have a good mix of leaf shapes—some tall strap-shaped leaves such as those of cordylines, yuccas, and irises help to punctuate the more fussy feel of small-leaved perennials like potentillas and hebes, for example.

Clean shapes and good foliage colour provide a backdrop for the flower colour and there is a range of shrubs (see pages116-119) that require relatively little maintenance. In an island bed, you can put the bigger shrubs in the centre.

For a backed border, they will stand behind smaller perennials, forming a quiet backdrop. Alternatively, choose perennials that are tough, sturdy, and require little staking and mix them with grasses for a border with a much more natural appearance.

SUMMER BORDER

The border in summer in a garden in Holland, where natural-style borders predominate. The planting flows very naturally and the colours intermingle, much as nature would intend. This style of planting works particularly well in large cottage gardens.

TRADITIONAL BORDER PLAN

This traditional border plan has 13 perennials, some of which, like the penstemons, lupins and delphiniums, will require staking. To create an easier to maintain version, you will need to reduce the variety of plants, employing a couple of shrubs and changing some of the perennials to ones that require minimum maintenance. A low-maintenance version of this plan is shown on the opposite page.

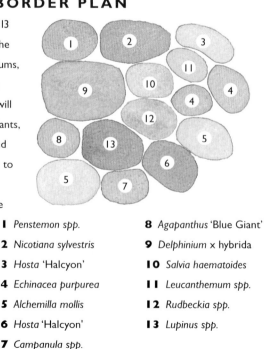

1 *Penstemon spp.*
2 *Nicotiana sylvestris*
3 *Hosta* 'Halcyon'
4 *Echinacea purpurea*
5 *Alchemilla mollis*
6 *Hosta* 'Halcyon'
7 *Campanula spp.*
8 *Agapanthus* 'Blue Giant'
9 *Delphinium* x hybrida
10 *Salvia haematoides*
11 *Leucanthemum spp.*
12 *Rudbeckia spp.*
13 *Lupinus spp.*

LOW-MAINTENANCE FLOWER AND FOLIAGE BORDER

To achieve an easier to care for border, you need to reduce the variety of plants while including a couple of shrubs that require little or no maintenance. These will bulk out the border and add structure without adding to the work. Aim to achieve a good balance of foliage and flowers, ideally with some evergreen foliage for year-round interest.

There are a number of good evergreen shrubs to choose from (see pages 116-7) and those with a spreading habit, like some forms of juniper and viburnum, are ideal. Aim to choose interesting leaf shapes that make a contrast of texture to compensate for the fact that there will not be as much vivid flower colour.

1 *Hebe* '**Midsummer Beauty**'
Evergreen. Long flowering season. Minimal pruning.

2 *Echinacea purpurea*
Sturdy stemmed perennial. No staking. Cut down after flowering.

3 *Salvia haematoides* '**Indigo**'
No staking. Cut down to basal leaves after flowering.

4 *Santolina chamaecyparissus*
Evergreen. Cut hard back every 2-3 years.

5 *Hosta* '**Halcyon**'
Maintenance-free.

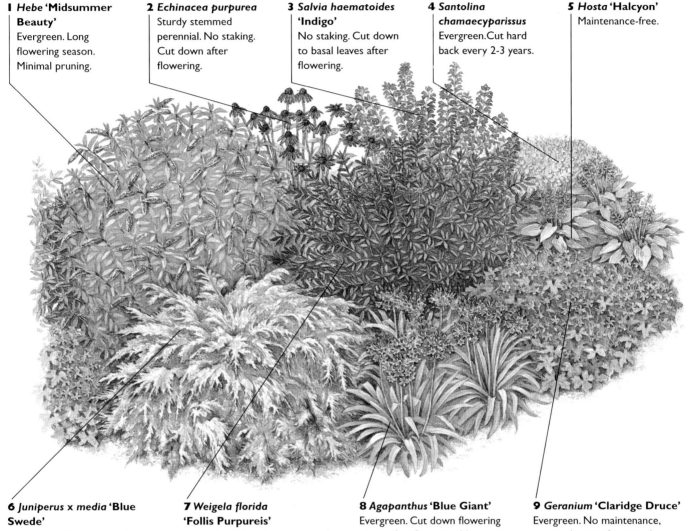

6 *Juniperus* x *media* '**Blue Swede**'
Evergreen with spreading habit. Maintenance-free.

7 *Weigela florida* '**Follis Purpureis**'
Prune flowering stems only each year.

8 *Agapanthus* '**Blue Giant**'
Evergreen. Cut down flowering stems after flowering. No staking.

9 *Geranium* '**Claridge Druce**'
Evergreen. No maintenance, except division if it spreads too far.

FLOWER AND FOLIAGE BORDER PLAN

Plants have been whittled down, but good low-maintenance performers have been retained, such as the thistle (*Echinacea purpurea*), the architectural-looking *Hosta* 'Halcyon', and the pretty blue-flowered Agapanthus and salvias which are relatively easy to grow. It includes evergreens for all-year interest..

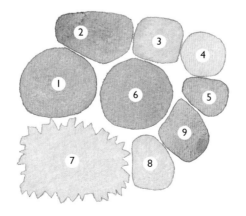

1 *Hebe* 'Midsummer Beauty' x 1

2 *Echinacea purpurea* x 3

3 *Salvia haematoides* 'Indigo' x 3

4 *Santolina chamaecyparissus* x 1

5 *Hosta* 'Halcyon' x 3

6 *Juniperus* x *media* 'Blue Swede' x 1

7 *Weigela florida* 'Folliis Purpureis' x 1

8 *Agapanthus* 'Blue Giant' x 3

9 *Geranium* 'Claridge Druce' x 3

PUTTING A DESIGN
INTO PRACTICE

This case study of a typical long, narrow urban garden demonstrates how

a new low-maintenance design can be created in easy stages, as and when you

have the time to carry out the work.

A LONG, NARROW plot is never the easiest to deal with in design terms, because there is so little natural variety in the vista that lies ahead of you. When Ian and Lydia Sidaway first acquired this garden, it was laid out in the traditional manner with a long rectangle of grass, surrounded by flower borders—pleasant enough but unexciting visually.

Being a painter, Ian decided that it would be good to have a studio at the end of the garden and so, when thinking about redesigning the garden, this was the first design priority. He also wanted to create visual interest throughout the length of the garden, rather than simply at the sides.

Like most us with busy lives, he could spare only a certain amount of time for the garden, and he decided to tackle the design in pieces, rather than as one composite piece of work. His staging process was an interesting piece of lateral thinking and the design was one of 'nibbling away' at the existing framework rather than completely revamping it, as a professional garden designer might have done.

In arriving at the solutions he has chosen, he was very much influenced

by formal French gardens, in particular one at Bonnieux in Provence which makes marvellous use of clipped evergreens, and another in Belgium by the internationally renowned garden

designer Walda Pairon, who mixes formal and informal shapes to great effect in her own town garden. Without deliberately planning to create a low-maintenance garden, his design choices

RIGHT The garden as it was originally, with its single wide expanse of lawn with borders formally arranged on either side. The garden looks (as it is) long and narrow.

ABOVE The next part of the garden to be renewed was the end, where the studio was built. A small continental style gravel patio was constructed with a short gravel path, bordered by beds leading towards the next area.

BELOW Finally, a new deck was created next to the house, which effectively bridges the house and garden. Laying a deck over is the easiest way to deal with changes of level, as steps can be incorporated easily.

TOP In the first stage the centre part of the garden was tackled, in which the grass was cut away on the left to create a wider square border and a small crazy-paved sitting area created.

ABOVE The second part of the garden to be constructed was the area beyond the gravel patio in which the lawn was cut away to incorporate new beds and a small brick-paved patio.

are nevertheless low-maintenance in practice, since both the surfaces and the planting are extremely easy to maintain. He has, in fact, followed the low-maintenance dictum of creating hard surfaces, but mixing them to add interest, so that at the studio end of the garden, there is an expanse of gravel. Halfway down the garden there is a brick patio area and close to the house, a deck has been made to cope with the original change in level between house and garden. These surfaces each have a slightly different character, with subtle differences in the planting style.

The plants have been chosen for their form, foliage interest, and year-round appeal. Although Ian clips the evergreens, particularly the box and the privet, he reckons it takes very little time and he simply snips off the new shoots and tidies them up when passing them. In fact, all his garden chores are carried out in this simple, ad hoc manner, which is one the experts recommend as the most effective means to keep a garden under control.

On flowering plants (of which Ian has only a few) it is ideal, since pruning after flowering ensures that you do not snip off next year's flowering wood by mistake—a common error made by over-enthusiastic pruners!

With a garden a third of the size of Ian's, you could opt for one element of the scheme alone, or, with a more traditional long rectangle, you could take two of the elements, rather than all three.

Eventually Ian plans to get rid of the grass altogether, but it is taking less and less time to mow. The stepping stones that provide the path down its centre are set lower than the surface of the surrounding grass so the mower simply runs over the top of them.

As he found out, grass isn't an ideal solution if you make continuous journeys across it, as it rapidly becomes worn, and in gardens with high trees on either side, the grass growth is likely to be patchy and uneven from lack of light.

Among Ian's favourite plants are

LEFT AND FAR LEFT The central area of the garden looking towards the studio with the planting fully grown. The use of evergreens makes the garden easy to care for. Mixing their shape and form adds interest, since without this element of shaping the foliage might look overly dense and heavy. Scale is also an important element (see inset picture of the left hand side of the border), as is the use of contrasting foliage forms and sizes to create additional interest. These are all very valuable lessons to learn when planning low-maintenance planting because you have fewer choices at your disposal and must therefore learn to make the best possible design use of a more limited selection of plants at your disposal.

small-leaved evergreens for clipping such as box (*Buxus sempervirens*) and privet (*Ligustrum ovalifolium*). These make neat mounds that contrast well with the tall, pencil-thin conifers, such as cypresses and junipers, so that not only do you get contrast of size but also of form and texture. This is important with evergreens, which can otherwise appear too dense.

To create variety in leaf shape and form, big-leaved perennials like *Gunnera manicata* contrast with smaller leaves like those of the smoke bush (*Cotinus coggygria*) and berberis, with its arching sprays of fine little leaves. Sprawling plants like *Santolina chamaecyparissus* and creeping junipers, such as *Juniperus procumbens* help to create a strong horizontal line against which standards of rosemary in pots make interesting verticals.

Originally, Ian created a small vegetable garden near the studio to grow some of his favourite edible plants. He has a particular passion for courgette flowers (dipped in batter) and as these are among the easiest vegetables to grow, he found he had a ready supply for very little work. He also likes to grow salad crops—rocket being among the easiest.

PLANTING SUGGESTIONS

Abies koreana
Acer griseum
Berberis x stenophylla
Buxus sempervirens
Catalpa bignonioides
Choisya ternata
Cupressus sempervirens
Elaeagnus commutata
Eriobotrya japonica
Euphorbia characias
Gunnera manicata
Juniperus communis 'Hibernica'
Lonicera nitida
Mahonia aquifolium
Pittosporum tobira
Prunus laurocerasus 'Otto Luykens'
Rosmarinus officinalis
Picea pungens
Salvia officinalis 'Purpurascens'
Santolina chamaecyparissus
Skimmia japonica
Taxus baccata
Viburnum macrophylla
Viburnum tinus

LEFT Balls of box and *Lonicera nitida* make a marvellous contrast against the tall yew and bright foliage of the *Pieris*.

BELOW RIGHT The small, glossy leaves of a laurel contrast with the spikier foliage of a young juniper.

BELOW LEFT Sempervivums and sedums need little watering.

OPPOSITE This garden shows how form is as important as colour in design.

JAPANESE-STYLE GARDEN

Water, gravel, stones and evergreen plants in simply laid-out designs are the hallmarks of Japanese style gardens, and are a good solution for an easy-to-care-for city garden.

THE GARDEN FEATURED on these pages was first made more than 30 years ago in Holland. While it is not a classical Japanese garden, it is strongly influenced by the Japanese design preference for harmony of materials and simplicity of design and a concentration on form and texture rather than on colour. The latter has long been the chief aim of any Western-inspired garden but to create a garden in the Japanese style, you need to abandon any previously held notions about needing a riot of colour. It is the antithesis of the hanging basket school of gardening. You need first to remove any unnecessary features and simplify the design and the planting to well-chosen shrubs and trees, in the main, that have excellent form. Evergreens are the best value, because they retain their shape and structure through the year, especially those that are slow-growing with a neat habit. To

ABOVE LEFT A stepping stone bridge provides a perfect place to stand and contemplate the reflections in the pool.

RIGHT Contrasting foliage forms and textures are one of the hallmarks of Japanese design. Simplicity is the key, as this understated design with its central gravelled area amply demonstrates. Choosing slow-growing evergreens, like hebes, junipers, and viburnums, provides good contrast of shape with very little pruning needed.

LOW-MAINTENANCE FEATURES

ORNAMENTAL SHRUB
Improves visual appearance, needs no maintenance

YEW HEDGE
Slow-growing needs only occasional clipping

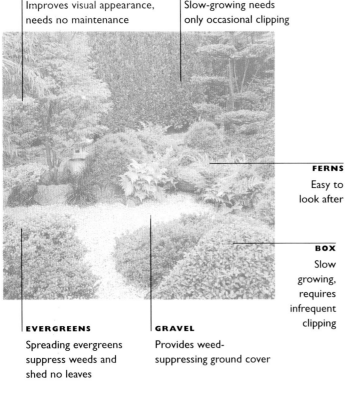

FERNS
Easy to look after

BOX
Slow growing, requires infrequent clipping

EVERGREENS
Spreading evergreens suppress weeds and shed no leaves

GRAVEL
Provides weed-suppressing ground cover

BELOW The elegant, rounded leaves of waterlilies spread out over deeper water in the large pool, its edges disguised with oriental-style boulders and rocks among which damp-loving ferns and reeds flourish.

RIGHT The view of the pool with its changes of level and naturally planted surrounds. Japanese maples, rhododendrons, and pines flourish around its perimeters, while a yew hedge provides an evergreen backdrop.

prevent the planting from looking dull, choose forms and shapes that contrast well, so that they set each other off.

Once you focus on the foliage, you realize that gardens do not necessarily need flower colour to gain interest, and the shape and form is far better appreciated when the eye is not distracted by lurid flowers. The removal of spotty colour creates a feeling of calm restfulness, which is very much in keeping with the Japanese idea of

harmony and balance. The foliage tends to be evergreen and small, with rounded shapes contrasting with the more wiry outline of small trees, such as dwarf pines. Trees that are frequently used in Japanese style gardens include the smaller pines, such as the dwarf mountain pine (*Pinus mugo*), little maples like *Acer japonicum dissectum* 'Atropurpureum', with its bronze, finely divided leaves, and the shrubby dwarf black spruce (*Picea mariana* ' Nana').

Good evergreen shrubs include *Viburnum davidii*, with its neat dome shape of dark green leaves (to about 1.5m/5ft) and *Hebe cupressoides*, which grows to about 1.2m (4ft) high and wide.

Clipping is a feature in Japanese gardens, and although this might seem contrary to a low-maintenance approach, it is not done frequently (provided you choose slow-growing plants) and can usually be dealt within two weekends in summer (unlike a

ABOVE The rounded leaves of waterlilies (*Nymphea*) make an attractive feature and need relatively little care.

ABOVE Ferns, with their finely divided foliage, make a good textural contrast to small, dark-leaved evergreens.

ABOVE The rich, bronze-purple foliage of the Japanese maple brings a touch of colour to an otherwise monochromatic scheme.

lawn which takes weekly maintenance).

There are two principal elements in any Japanese-inspired garden, and they are both included in this one. One is water; the other is gravel: the 'yin' of flowing water to counterbalance the 'yang' of the stone. Flowing, reflective, calm and clear, water also brings the garden to life visually, balancing out the hard edges created by pebbles, boulders and stones. Again, none of it, once installed, is time-consuming to maintain. If you can create a large area of water, as in the garden shown here , it is worth including a stepping stone bridge from which to pause and enjoy the reflections. It is also good idea to create deeper and shallower areas of water, as water-loving plants have different preferences. In deep, still water (over 1m/3ft in depth), you can grow water lilies, the archetypal symbol of the Japanese garden, with their handsome evergreen rounded leaves and elegant, waxy flowers. In the shallower margins, Japanese iris (*I. ensata*) will flourish, their tall, sword-shaped leaves and their broader, slightly flatter flag-like flowers.

Carefully placed ornament is also a feature of Japanese style gardens, from the simplicity of a boulder strategically placed at a focal point to stone lanterns or statues. Again, the key is to opt for less, not more, and to position the ornaments so that they offset the planting.

SEMI-WILD GARDEN

One way to cut down on maintenance is to create a sympathetic bridge between wild plants and cultivated ones. The Priona garden in Holland is an example worth following.

Including a wild garden in a book on low-maintenance gardens is, perhaps, stretching the point a bit, since a truly wild garden is not a garden at all, but much depends on the degree of control you wish to exercise over the planting, and how determined you are to ensure that the plants that you prefer take precedence over those that you do not.

Much depends, too, on your ability to understand the conditions in which you are gardening, since different plants flourish in particular climates and soil conditions, and some make reasonable relationships with each other, while others are more likely to try to control the show. A wild garden on alkaline soil will have a very different look to one on acid soil, and for the garden to be as low-maintenance as possible, you need to encourage those plants that enjoy the conditions, so no wild garden planting can be automatically copied across the board. Preliminary research, and some expert advice, will be needed before you begin.

This garden in Holland, belonging to Henk Gerritsen (which he designed together with his late partner, Anton Schlepers), is an interesting mixture of wild and controlled planting, with many plants allowed to self-seed and construct their own redesign of the planting scheme each year. Committed community garden enthusiasts, with a strong interest in ecologically friendly gardens, Henk and Anton moved to this three-and-a-half-acre (1.5 hectare) garden at Priona in rural Overjisell, where they had space to experiment with a style of gardening that is relaxed within an controlled framework. Interestingly,

LOW-MAINTENANCE FEATURES

HEDGES
Slow growing, need only occasional clipping

TREES
Provide shady habitat and structure for the naturalized planting beneath

SELF-SEEDING PERENNIALS
Plants like Verbascum perpetuate themselves by naturalizing

RELAXED PLANTING
Tightly packed, sturdy perennials need no staking

GRAVEL PATH
Needs no weeding, relaxed appearance appropriate for planting

ABOVE LEFT A scarecrow rises above heads of wild parsnip.

RIGHT The wilder elements of the perennial planting, with verbascums, *Artemisia absinthium* and *Origanum*, left to self-seed at will, are contained in a more formal enclosure of clipped hedging, creating a balance between control and nature, effort and ease.

Anton and Henk approached gardening from very different viewpoints and preferences: of the two, Henk believed more strongly in environmental issues; Anton loved certain plants and flowers and carried on planting his chosen cultivars, regardless of Henk's more rigidly controlled preferences. Gardening itself is a struggle between gardener and nature and it is the balance that is struck (with neither one or the other winning) that makes gardens interesting and exciting. In Henk's and Anton's garden, this struggle was played out in microcosm as well as macrocosm, which is why the garden is vibrant, unusual, interesting, and, above all, fun. Following Anton's death, Henk has tried to carry this duality on, aware of how valuable it has been in preventing the garden from becoming boring and predictable.

Not all the garden is given over to wild planting—a portion of it contains some eccentrically shaped topiary which has an almost wave-like appearance— nor is it all by any means low-maintenance, but the underlying philosophy is to allow nature to take its course within a fairly controlled overall framework and to let unusual or interesting things to happen, so that the gardener is not as much the all-powerful controller, as in so many manicured Western gardens, but more the conductor of a slightly unruly orchestra!

A major feature of this garden is the way in which different areas have been dedicated to different forms of natural planting. There is, for example, a shady border near the house with ground-covering sweeps of geraniums (always a good choice for low-maintenance borders), nepeta and tradescantia. Another border contains a mixed display of giant perennials, including the American *Eupatorium maculatum*, asters and various big daisies. The big perennials are tightly packed and need no staking. Henk Gerritsen also prefers to leave the plants uncut until spring, to get the benefit throughout the winter from the skeleton outlines of browned, dessicated stems and leaves, and various seedheads.

Another portion has been dedicated to a wild flower meadow. Although this sounds like the low-maintenance gardener's idea of heaven—flower colour with almost no mowing— creating and maintaining the right balance of flowers to grasses is not as simple as it sounds. Flowering meadows require poor soil if the flowers are to flourish and the more aggressive weeds are to be prevented from taking precedence.

If you want to create a flowery meadow, be aware that this is not a truly low-maintenance option, although the work is concentrated into two or three 'hits' each year. Remember that for meadow flowers to flourish, the soil needs to be poor, otherwise invasive weeds will take over. You can buy packeted mixtures of grasses and wild flowers for sowing in autumn.

According to Henk, when you start off a wild flower meadow, it will generally be full of spring-flowering plants, and you mow the area twice a year, once in high summer and once in autumn. The grass must never be cut too short (about 8cm/3in) and any mowings need to be removed to prevent the fertility of the soil getting too rich. (If you have a large garden, rent a riding mower for the grass-cutting and gathering operations). Once the fertility starts to decline, the number of summer-flowering plants will increase, and your meadow will start to have both a spring- and summer-flowering season. Mowing can be cut to once a year. This takes about 10 years to happen, so wild meadows are not for those dedicated to instant gardens.

LEFT A gravel path meanders through the loose island beds with self-supporting perennials chosen for their dramatic vertical interest.

PLANT LIST

NATURALIZING FLOWERS
Artemisia absinthium
Aster umbellatus
Cephalaria gigantea
Lamium orvala
Meconopsis cambrica
Origanum vulgare
Salvia glutinosa
Scorzonera hispanica
Silene vulgaris
Stachys officinalis
Telekia speciosa
Thalictrum aquilegiifolium.
T. delavayi
T. polygamum

MEADOW GRASSES
Agrimonia eupatoria
Cirsium heterophyllum
Daucus carota
Galium mollugo
Geranium pratense
Hypericum perforatum
Hypochaeris radicata
Leucanthemum vulgare
Malva moschata
Senecio erucifolius.
S. jacobaea
Trapopogon pratensis

ABOVE The wildflower meadow with grasses, yarrow (*Achillea millefolium*), and wild mullein (*Verbascum officinalis*).

LEFT A shady corner plays host to some undemanding plants, including the statuesque macleaya, with its handsome gray green leaves and bronze-coloured plumes of flowers.

URBAN JUNGLE

Some sites, and some climates, are more demanding than others. This garden, only four miles from the sea, has to cope with salt, wind, and fog, while still being easy to look after.

A SMALL PLOT (only 8 x 18m/ 30 x 60ft), this urban garden in San Francisco is the work of Sonny Garcia and his partner, Tom, and is a masterpiece in deception, since there is no way you get a true picture of its limitations of size. The secret, according to Sonny, lies in the fact that changes of level have been introduced both by creating decks and by using containers for the plants. He also believes that no matter how small the garden, you should never be able to see it all, from any angle. He wanted to create an air of mystery and suspense, as the eye wanders around and discovers unexpected features hidden at first glance by the tapestry of foliage.

His solutions to creating height in the garden are varied, and he decided to structure the site with five different levels. The changes are gradual, ranging from one step between levels to a six-step staircase to a raised back deck, which is used as a place to relax and also to view the rest of the garden.

The garden also includes two water features, one a pond and waterfall in a shady area of the garden, the surroundings hidden among palms and ferns. Another is a spouting oriental urn, sited under a pergola, over which climbing plants are grown to create interest at yet another level.

The planting in the garden is heavily dependent on foliage plants with good leaf colour. Sonny has picked those with interesting variegations, or with purple or golden foliage, to create a brilliant display without having to

ABOVE LEFT Stone masks make an unusual pathway.

RIGHT Changes of level and lush planting disguise the limited space of this small urban plot. There are contrasts of foliage colour and texture, with the sharp fans of the palm in the foreground and the strappy leaves of cordylines and phormiums providing structure. Climbers like *Clematis montana* (on the right) blur the boundaries while the big trumpet flowers of daturas (*Brugmansia*) add an element of theatricality.

LOW-MAINTENANCE FEATURES

LARGE EVERGREENS
Provide easy structure for the garden

DECKED AREAS
Allow space for relaxation

EVERGREEN SHRUBS
Mixed shrub foliage provides colour and variety with less effort than perennial flowers

CLIMBERS
Cling to walls and blur boundaries

RAISED AREAS
Provide a place to show off and care for small plants easily

CLOSE PLANTING
Helps to suppress weeds

resort to flower colour. Strikingly architectural plants, like the purple-leaved cordyline, *C. australis* 'Purpurea', *Phormium tenax,* and the windmill palm (*Trachycarpus fortunei*) contrast with smaller-leaved forms, like the dark-leaved berberis and fuchsias. The use of coloured evergreen foliage plants makes the garden much easier to maintain (less deadheading and general pruning) while ensuring it does not lack vibrancy. Ferns and grasses are good low-maintenance plants with handsome forms. The planting is dense and lush, its variety of colour, height, size, and shape preventing it from becoming gloomy or forbidding. Pruning is needed but can be kept to a once or twice a year annual blitz.

Apart from the decking for the different levels, paving stones and pebbles provide low-maintenance surfacing for walkways and paths. Garden ornaments—stone balls, mirrors, and sculptures—add interest and variety without adding to the overall workload of the garden.

ABOVE Closely packed foliage plants surround the bench, creating a neatly tiered effect, with the cordyline playing the dominant role.

LEFT A shady path, overhung with shrubs and flanked with grasses, provides a glimpse of the sitting area beyond.

RIGHT The pretty daisy-flowered *Felicia amelloides* sprawls lazily over a wire-frame chair doubling as a plant support.

In exposed urban areas where strong winds and pollution are a problem, choosing plants that can withstand wind and are tolerant of acid rain is essential. Among good candidates for these kind of situations are the evergreens *Escallonia rubra* and *Griselinia littoralis*, both of which make good evergreen screens and windbreaks, and will cope with salt spray in coastal gardens, as will the deciduous buddlejas, fuchsias, and spiraeas.

SUBURBAN SIMPLICITY

*Larger gardens can be made easier to maintain by introducing areas that
require less work than the rest of the garden. This New Zealand garden has
a low-maintenance walkway and easy-to-care-for terraces.*

NOT EVERYONE NEEDS or wants to create an entirely low-maintenance garden, but finding ways to introduce low-maintenance ideas into the overall design can give you the opportunity to spend the time you do have on areas of particular interest. If, for example, you are determined to keep a small lawn, then you could possibly consider less time-consuming solutions for other parts of the garden.

In this garden in New Zealand, a shady area has been devoted to a low-maintenance pathway and borders using foliage planting, stepping stones and low-growing, mat-forming ground cover. This plan would work well, too, for a much smaller, shady city garden, culminating with perhaps

a small patio area at the far end and with a terrace (see overleaf) close to the house itself. Good plants for underfoot planting are thymes and chamomiles in sunny areas and baby's tears (*Soleirolia soleirolii*) and *Ajuga reptans* in shadier ones.

If you opt for generally low-maintenance surfaces and planting, you can afford to give the area an element of controlled formality with neatly regimented clipped evergreens (a solution that has worked equally well in the garden featured on pages 62-67). Clipping evergreens is not as time-consuming as it might appear, provided you opt for the slow-growing small leaved types, such as boxwood (*Buxus sempervirens*), which

will only demand clipping twice a year. A faster growing evergreen, such as privet, will need clipping at least twice as often to keep it looking neat.

Standards are much the same: once trained, they require only minimal clipping, providing you pick appropriate plants. Myrtle (*Myrus communis*) is a good choice for warmer climates, with its aromatic foliage. Rosemary (also half-hardy) can be trained similarly into mop-headed standards, as can some forms of argyranthemum, for example.

Another good solution in a small urban garden is to create a mini-arboretum at one end of the garden, with a few relatively small ornamental trees, such as hawthorns (*Crataegus*)

LOW-MAINTENANCE FEATURES

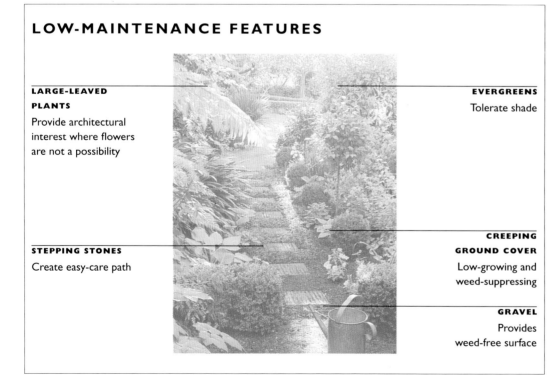

LARGE-LEAVED PLANTS
Provide architectural interest where flowers are not a possibility

STEPPING STONES
Create easy-care path

EVERGREENS
Tolerate shade

CREEPING GROUND COVER
Low-growing and weed-suppressing

GRAVEL
Provides weed-free surface

RIGHT
In this shady area of the garden, low-maintenance planting and a pathway help cut down on the work. A mixture of shrubs and perennials, grown mostly for their foliage, line each side of the path, which is a simple gravel, ground cover, and stepping stone combination.

and birch (*Betula*) creating light dappled shade, in which you can grow some ground-covering woodland plants, like brunnera, tellima and symphytum, which will spread rapidly in the right conditions to provide weed-suppressing ground cover.

Near the house, the patio areas and terraces are best planted with fairly tough, drought-resistant plants in pots. If you groups the plants together, you help to reduce water loss and you also make it easier to carry out any watering needed. Herbs like lavender and rosemary can be clipped into formal shapes, as can santolina and box. They are all very tolerant of dry soil and need only infrequent watering.

Self-clinging climbers, such as *Parthenocissus henryana* or *Hydrangea petiolaris* can cover the walls. Small tables are the ideal place to show off collections of succulents, which again are extremely undemanding, requiring very little attention but repaying you with year-round interest.

ABOVE A shade-loving combination of *Euphorbia amygdaloides*, and the climbing hydrangea, *Hydrangea petiolaris*, predominating.

LEFT On the patio, containers of neatly clipped evergreens, grown as topiary shapes and standards, provide a year-round feature. Once trained, the plants only need clipping twice a year to keep them in shape.

RIGHT Grouped pots and raised containers make this summery terrace easier to look after. Tender plants, like the little lemon tree, will need overwintering indoors in colder climates.

COUNTRY STUDIO

This country garden is an exciting blend of modern design and traditional naturalistic planting that also happens to be surprisingly low-maintenance.

THIS GARDEN PROVIDES an interesting marriage of low-maintenance ideas; the deck surrounding is simply planted with occasional large pots of specimen plants while the naturalistic planting beyond it comprises broad sweeps of big herbaceous perennials.

Home of garden designer Anthony Paul, the garden embodies his interest in modern design and ecological trends. He himself gave up working in the city to work from the much more congenial surroundings of his 16th-century cottage, and the studio was built to accommodate his practice. The garden lies in a secluded river valley on the Surrey and Sussex borders in England—it comprises a vast 10 acres

(4 hectares), much of which is woodland garden in which his Dutch wife, Hannah Peschar, exhibits her collection of modern sculpture.

The area surrounding Anthony's studio is not only easy to maintain: it is also a haven for wildlife. Damp-loving wild flowers flourish beside the stream that runs through the garden, among them the common Himalayan balsam (*Impatiens glandulifera*) and rosebay willowherb (*Epilobium angustifolium*), and the monkey flower (*Mimulus guttatus*).

In the river and its pools, water lilies and 'floating heart' (*Nymphaea peltata*) display their handsome leaves. At the edges of the river grows a range of damp-loving perennials, including

the marginal aquatics like bulrushes (*Typha angustifolia*) and the soft rush (*Juncus effusus*). One of Anthony's favourite plants is the huge South American *Gunnera manicata* which copes surprisingly well with a temperate climate provided it has some shelter. None of these plants requires much in the way of maintenance, but once a year or so over-vigorous elements need to be divided and cut back to prevent them from taking over entirely. The secret

LOW-MAINTENANCE FEATURES

DRIFTS OF PERENNIALS
Relaxed, low-maintenance planting

LARGE POTS
Easy to maintain if planted with year-round evergreens

DECKING
Easy-care surface for change of level

GRAVEL
Easy-care surface

lies in choosing plants (or allowing them to self-seed naturally) so that the selection is entirely appropriate for the place. This automatically halves the gardener's work.

Along the river banks you can catch a glimpse of a whole host of insects and butterflies in their ideal habitat. Kingfishers can be seen darting up the river while wrens and robins nest in the overhanging trees. The river teems with fish, including golden rudd, and coots call from the reed beds. The great joy of a natural country garden is the encouragement it gives to local wildlife, and creating suitable havens is not particularly time-consuming; it simply requires some knowledge of their preferred habitats.

Closer to the studio, Anthony Paul has opted for large-scale drifts of strikingly contrasted colours: yellow and purple, or bright yellow with burnt orange, are both particularly effective. By growing the plants in huge drifts, he avoids the need for any staking or deadheading. His planting schemes include *Ligularia* 'The Rocket' with its spires of golden yellow flowers placed

TOP The front entrance to the studio with its neatly gravelled surface and decked steps. Large terracotta pots of box and a dwarf pine create an easy-to-care-for formal feature, in contrast to the relaxed drifts of perennials beyond.

RIGHT The small terrace deck overhangs the pool below, in which naturalized plants that enjoy damp conditions create a semi-wild habitat for the local flora and fauna.

LEFT Small pots of clipped small-leaved, slow-growing box create a formal touch above the wilder drifts of ligularias, with their golden pokers of small flowers and filigree foliage.

RIGHT Huge perennial drifts surround the studio, in this view two different ligularias, *Helenium* 'Moerheim Beauty' and *Thalictrum delavayi* behind.

BELOW Small Chinese pots make ideal small water gardens; in this case, for a giant rush.

next to *Telekia speciosa*, with its characteristic large, daisy-like, rich golden flower heads, and large clumps of *Helenium* 'Butterpat' with its bright yellow daisies next to *Silphium laciniatum*. In the background, soft purple banks of *Thalictrum*

rochebruneanum with its delicate foliage and flowers creates a misty backdrop. Equally effective are combination plantings of *Helianthus* x *multiflorus* 'Soleil d'Or' with the dramatic purple blue flower heads of *Cynara cardunculus* and soft, grayish-green *Macleaya microcarpa* with its delicate coral pink plumes of flowers against the deep burnt orange of *Helenium* 'Moerheim Beauty'.

The decking around Anthony's studio was created from reclaimed Iroko timber, while the supporting timber was constructed from the storm-damaged trees in Anthony's own garden.

To create focal points on the deck, large, deep blue pots from Thailand have been filled with water and planted with the vigorous water plant, *Pontederia lancifolia*, with its spear-shaped, bright green leaves and spires of brilliant blue flowers, or the attractive Eygptian papyrus, *Cyperus papyrus*.

EASIER WAYS TO GARDEN

Apart from planning a more low-maintenance design for your garden, you also need to find ways to cut down on the work. This chapter discusses the ways in which you can minimize labour in the garden by sensible organization of the workload, and by ensuring that you go about the garden tasks in the least time-consuming ways. Every aspect of plant and garden maintenance is included, from choosing appropriate tools to simpler ways to prune.

TOOLS AND EQUIPMENT

In order to carry out basic maintenance work in the garden efficiently you will need a few basic tools and items of equipment. It pays to invest in as good quality tools as you can afford, as these will be easier to use, more reliable, and more robust, saving you effort in the long term.

MECHANIZING AS MANY of your garden tasks as possible can reduce the time spent working, and increase the time spent relaxing in the garden instead.

But before deciding which pieces of equipment are essential, you need to assess which are your most common a tasks in a garden and how versatile certain tools might be—if one tool can be used for several jobs, it's probably worth investing in.

The following tools are the most frequently used in the garden and it is worth buying the best-quality items you can afford, since a few well-made items will be more comfortable to use, will last longer and will do a better job.

GARDEN ESSENTIALS

A good spade and fork are vital. Use the spade for digging, breaking up the ground, and lifting soil, the fork for general cultivation, planting, lifting plants, and controlling weeds.

A rake is a must for evening out the soil before planting, breaking up the soil, making seed drills, and general tidying. A good, strong pair of secateurs is also invaluable for cutting through woody stems, such as when pruning, and for removing dead flowers. Use a trowel for digging holes and planting smaller plants and bulbs, as well as for working in containers and raised beds. A fan rake is good for removing moss and aerating a lawn, if you have one, as well as for raking up leaves and general garden debris. A good pair of shears are invaluable, particularly if you have hedges that require trimming.

Two more useful items to add to the list are a good, stiff broom, which is useful for sweeping paths and paved areas, and a robust garden knife for general use.

USEFUL EQUIPMENT

There are many tools that can be classed as useful, but if you only use a specific piece of equipment once or twice a year, it may well prove much more cost effective and convenient to rent it for a few days after stockpiling the work for which it's needed. For example, only a garden with plenty of roses, trees and shrubs can truly justify

BASIC TOOLS

The tools shown here represent the basic kit you will need. Keep tools with sharp blades oiled and rust-free, and keep all tools under cover when not in use.

Shears

Garden knife

Spade

Fork

Rake

Trowel

Secateurs

HANDY EQUIPMENT

What you need in the way of other equipment depends to some extent on the style of garden. If you have a lawn, you will need a good lawnmower: electric rotary mowers do not cut the finest lawns, but they are the most practical in the low-maintenance garden. A good well-balanced wheelbarrow is usually essential in larger gardens, and spraying equipment is useful for both weedkilling and for foliage feeds.

Wheelbarrow

Hand spray

Lawn mower

Pump spray

applying liquid feeds. Choose a well-balanced watering can that starts to pour as soon as it is tilted, with a long spout for extra reach.

You will almost certainly need to spray your plants, either to apply weedkillers or pesticides, to mist the leaves with water, or to apply a foliar feed. You can either use a simple hand-held spray, or a more sophisticated pump action spray if you have a large area to cover.

Loppers or a saw are useful for pruning branches and stems that are too thick for secateurs. Hoes are handy for cultivating top soil, weeding around plants, and for creating seed drills. A wheelbarrow is useful for collecting garbage and moving heavier materials, while an electric mower is a great labour-saving device if you have a small lawn.

Rotary mowers have much greater potential for the low-maintenance garden than cylinder mowers: they have far fewer moving parts (which reduces wear and tear); they are easier to sharpen; and they are much more versatile for cutting long or damp grass.

the gardener owning a shredder or chipper. For the rest, it is better to stockpile the prunings, and then feed them through a shredder that has been rented for the day—or, even better, share the cost with a neighbour. There are other items that you will use far more often. A good quality watering can or a hosepipe is useful for watering plants until they are established and for

GARDEN SAFETY

Where machinery is being used, it is always advisable to wear certain items of protective clothing in order to minimize any risk of injury. Even when the machinery and equipment being used is not particularly dangerous, it's still advisable to take precautions, as many accidents happen every year in the home in what appear to be safe circumstances.

For example, breaking up concrete with a hammer will almost certainly lead to stones and concrete chips flying as a result of the impact of hammer on concrete, and it is advisable to protect eyes with goggles. The most dangerous machine available for use in the garden is the chainsaw, and when using one, full safety equipment, including cut-proof trousers, should ALWAYS be worn.

BASIC SAFETY EQUIPMENT

Tough gardening gloves are vital for the gardener, as are goggles when using equipment such as shredders, trimmers or sprayers. Ear protectors will safeguard your ears while using noisy power tools, and a face mask should be worn for dusty, dirty or pesticide jobs.

Goggles

Ear protectors

Gloves

Face mask

PLANTING

Like children, plants need to get off to a good start. Choose strong young plants,

ensure the soil is in good condition and suitable for the chosen plant, and pay close attention

to the planting procedure to cut down on future maintenance.

IT IS IMPORTANT for the future health of your garden to ensure that you choose plants that are sound at the point of purchase (see right). You then need to ensure that you give them the best possible start. Contrary to what you actually see above ground, it is the root system of the plant that forms its powerhouse, and it should not be a case of out of sight, out of mind! The roots draw up their nutrients from the soil, and to do this they need not only the necessary nutrients but also moisture and, surprisingly, oxygen. If the soil is undug and very heavy, the fine roots of the plant will fail to do their work.

Your first task after purchase is to soak the plant in its pot in a bucket of water (and particularly if it has been supplied as a bare-root specimen) for enough time to ensure that it has replaced any water it may have lost at the point of sale. You then need to prepare the planting hole (see below).

Tempting though it is to scrape out a small hole and stuff the plant in, this will turn out to be a major mistake—even though you are obviously saving time in the short term! Time spent now on digging a hole large enough, adding fertilizer, and watering well will save you much time later in the plant's life.

Plants with tall or weak stems, or climbers, will need supporting both to train the plant in the right direction and to prevent windrock from damaging the roots. Make sure no plants are tied in too tight and replace ties as the plant grows. (See Reducing chores, pages 108-109.)

CHOOSING A HEALTHY PLANT

When you buy a plant from a nursery, try to choose one in good condition. It should look bushy rather than spindly (unless it is a single stemmed tree), the leaves should be healthy and unblemished, the surface of the pot should be weed and moss-free (if not, it has probably been in the pot too long), and the tips of the shoots should be fresh and green, not withered or brown. If you can, tip the plant upside down and make sure the roots are not growing out of the base (another sign it has been in the pot too long and may have become starved of food).

RIGHT A healthy young shrub, removed from its pot. The roots should not be too tightly wound round the soil. Before planting, tease the roots out gently.

Leaves in good condition

Healthy new shoots

Healthy roots

HOW TO PLANT

Whatever the size or type of plant, it needs a large planting hole. The reason for this is that turning over a large area of soil ensures that the soil is loose and aerated. The roots need space to extend, but they also need to be firmly anchored, so after planting make sure you firm the soil down around the plant. Generally, the rule is to dig a hole at least twice the size of the rootball, water it well and add fertilizer, insert the plant so that the crown of the rootball is just below the surface, backfill with the soil removed, water again, and firm down the soil.

1 Having dug the planting hole to an appropriate size, insert the plant, ensuring that the top of the rootball is just below the soil surface.

2 Once the plant (in this case a young climber) is securely planted, backfill the hole, water well and firm down with the heel of your boot.

KNOWING YOUR SOIL

In order for your plants to thrive, they must have the benefit of good soil. In the first place, you need to establish the kind of soil you have, since plants have adapted to particular conditions, and once you know the characteristics of your soil, you can choose plants that are appropriate, thereby cutting down on unnecessary feeding and watering.

Soils are classified according to the proportions of clay, silt or sand they contain. Sandy soils have little or no clay in them, which makes them very light and free-draining. Nutrients are quickly washed away and the soil can dry out, but they are easy to work.

Silty soils are more fertile and retain water better than sandy soils but they can be difficult to work and often form a surface crust or cap. This can cause problems, because rainwater runs off and fertilizers are not taken up so easily.

Clay soils are usually rich in nutrients and retain water well, but they are slow to drain, are prone to compaction, and can be difficult to work. The ideal is loam, a mixture of sand, silt, and clay. It has many of the better characteristics of all three, such as high fertility, good water-holding qualities, and good drainage. As well as these main soil types, there is also organic soil. Peat, as it is usually called, consists of thick layers of decomposed organic matter (such as leaves, grasses and moss). Peat soils often have poor drainage and lack useful nutrients. Certain plants, including those listed right, prefer a light, free-draining soil and will do particularly well in sandy soils, although you may have to add some well-rotted soil or manure to improve moisture retention.

Despite the fact that clay soil can be heavy and difficult to work, many plants will grow well in it because it is full of nutrients and holds water well, making it ideal for the plants listed.

THE pH OF SOIL

The other important consideration is the degree of acidity or alkalinity of the soil, which also affects the type of plants that you can grow.

Although most plants will grow in soil with a wide range of pH values, certain plants have specific requirements. Rhododendrons and many heathers, for example, only flourish in acid soils.

Before buying plants, check whether your soil is acid or alkaline and which plants grow best in such soil. You will always get the healthiest plants by opting for those that suit your conditions.

PLANTS FOR SPECIAL CONDITIONS

TREES & SHRUBS: *Brachyglottis, Calluna, Cistus, Coronilla Cytisus, Eucalyptus, Fuchsia, Gaultheria, Hebe, Helianthemum, Lonicera, Potentilla,* PERENNIALS: *Agapanthus, Alchemilla, Anthemis, Centranthus, Echinops, Eryngium, Kniphofia, Lupinus, Lychnis, Monarda, Papaver, Scabiosa, Verbascum*

PLANTS FOR CLAY SOIL

TREES & SHRUBS: *Aronia, Aucuba, Buddleja, Chaenomeles, Corylus, Escallonia, Euonymus, Ligustrum, Mahonia, Pyracantha, Ribes, Spiraea, Viburnum,* PERENNIALS: *Bergenia, Campanula, Delphinium, Geranium, Gypsophila, Helenium, Hemerocallis, Ligularia, Persicaria, Phlox, Ranunculus, Rudbeckia, Solidago, Thalictrum*

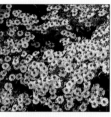
Helenium 'Gartensonne'

Pieris 'Forest Flame'

PLANTS FOR ACID SOIL

Acer palmatum, Camellia japonica, Cercidiphyllum japonicum, Cornus kousa, Epimedium grandiflorum, Kalmia latifolia, Liquidambar styradiflua, Pieris japonica, Rhododendron

PLANTS FOR ALKALINE SOIL

Anchusa azurea, Aquilegia vulgaris, Brunnera macrophylla, Kolkwitzia amabilis, Lonicera periclymenum, Morus nigra, Phlomis fruticosa, Syringa microphylla, Verbascum phoeniceum

Brunnera macrophylla

TESTING THE pH OF YOUR SOIL

You can determine the pH of your soil with an easy-to-use testing kit. These are widely available from nurseries and enable you to pinpoint exactly where your soil lies in the pH range. For an accurate indication of pH, read the results of your testing against the card provided with the kit.

ACID SOIL

A yellow or orange test result indicates that the soil is acid.

ALKALINE SOIL

A dark green or blue test result indicates alkaline soil.

FEEDING

Well-fed plants will reward you by growing stronger and staying healthier. Ensure that you give them the right food, at the right time, to cut down on long-term maintenance.

You MAY THINK you can get by without feeding your plants—one task too many—but a small amount of time and attention on appropriate feeding will save you time and trouble, as the plants will grow that much better and demand less of your time and attention later. A small amount on a regular basis is better than one huge meal, but one huge meal is better than none. Wiry plants that have adapted to poor soil (often those from the Mediterranean areas) demand less in the way of food and water than their large-leaved, fleshy cousins, so if you want to cut down on feeding, choose plants that have adapted for this purpose. If you want crops of fruit and large displays of flowers, attention to feeding cannot be ignored.

Plants manufacture their own food using sunlight, but in order to do this efficiently, their roots need to take up regular quantities of water and nutrients. The main elements, nitrogen, phosphorus, and potassium are required in large amounts; calcium, sulphur, and magnesium are needed in smaller quantities, while 'trace' elements, including boron, copper, iron, manganese, molybdenum, and zinc, are needed in minute measures.

In fertile soils, these nutrients are regularly replenished in the continuous cycle of plant death and decay. In a garden or container, they are unlikely to be present in sufficient amounts for healthy growth and fertilizer or manure will need to be added regularly. This is because the plants are more closely planted than they would be in the wild, and competition for nutrients is fierce.

Although many plants can grow quite satisfactorily for a number of years without adding any feed whatsoever, a lack of nutrients will ultimately have an effect. This may show up in disease-like symptoms as nutrients gradually become deficient, leading to distorted plant growth. More commonly, the growth rate of starved plants will very slowly decline, with flowers and fruits

RELEASE RATES	
FERTILIZER TYPE	PLANT RESPONSE
Slow-release (organic)	Improved growth over several years
Slow-release (resin-coated)	14-21 days
Quick-acting (top dressings)	7-10 days
Liquid feed (applied to soil)	5-7 days
Foliar feed	3-4 days

gradually getting smaller. This process is so slow that it may go unnoticed until the plants become so weak that they succumb to attack by pests and diseases.

PROVIDING AN ANNUAL FEED

For most roses and shrubs, a feed with a balanced all-purpose fertilizer once a year should be sufficient to maintain healthy growth and flowering. Plants that are regularly pruned once a year should be fed at a rate of 60g/sqm (2oz/sqyd) with a slow-release fertilizer that will release nutrients for a up to a year. Ornamental trees need a slightly stronger diet of 90g/sqm (3oz/sqyd). Woody plants such as these should be fed either immediately after the plant has been pruned, or in the spring. Herbaceous perennials will benefit from a feed of about 30g/sqm (1oz/sqyd) applied in early spring before growth starts, as this will reduce the risk of any fertilizer damaging the tender new foliage.

IMPROVING YOUR SOIL

It is a good idea to try to improve the quality of your soil by adding organic material to it, which will improve its ability to sustain plant growth. Adding

RIGHT To achieve the kind of flower power displayed here, you need to ensure that your plants are fed regularly. You will also need to ensure that they are regularly pruned, to encourage flower buds to form (see page 106).

APPLYING DRY AND LIQUID FERTILIZERS

Dry fertilizers are nutrients in a granular or pellet form, coated with a wax or resin compound that slowly dissolves and releases the fertilizer into the soil. The release can take from six to 18 months, depending on the thickness of the coating, soil moisture etc. Sprinkle fertilizer evenly over the soil and mix it into the top layer with a fork. If the soil is dry, water the area after application to dissolve the fertilizer and wash it down to the root zone.

Concentrated liquid fertilizer can be bought as either a liquid or a powder which is diluted in water and is applied to either the soil or leaves. If applying to the leaves, remember to do so early in the day or when it is cloudy, to avoid sun scorching the sprayed leaves.

APPLYING DRY FERTILIZER

Always apply evenly, following the directions given and avoid touching the foliage as the fertilizer can scorch plant leaves.

APPLYING LIQUID FERTILIZER

❶ Dilute liquid fertilizers with water and apply with a watering can or hosepipe. These feeds act fast to correct nutritional deficiencies.

❷ Apply as a foliar feed or to the soil at the base of the plant. Most foliar feeds are soil-acting, so any run-off is absorbed by the roots.

---

organic matter to light, free-draining soils will help them retain moisture, while adding organic matter to heavy clay soils will improve their aeration and oxygen content, making it easier for lighter-rooted plants to take hold.

There are two basic differences between fertilizers and manures: bulk and content. Fertilizers are used in relatively small quantities, because the nutrients they contain are concentrated. Manures are applied in larger amounts, as they provide only small quantities of major nutrients, but they do contain the added bonus of some minor nutrients and fibre which is slowly converted into valuable humus in the soil.

Some fertilizers are ideal for acting as a reviver, which makes them useful for helping plants to surge into growth or stop them from looking tired and straggly. These usually come in liquid form, which is generally safer to apply than dry fertilizer, as there is less risk of scorch and the plant absorbs liquid quickly.

The concentrated fertilizer can be either a liquid or a powder that is soluble when diluted in water. It can also be applied through a drip or sprinkler system, which cuts out more work. Avoid applying these fertilizers when rain is forecast, as they can be washed through the soil away from the plants' roots. Those fertilizers applied to the leaves of plants as a foliar feed are quickly absorbed by the leaves and are often applied as remedial feeds to overcome nutrient deficiencies. They have the advantage of working rapidly, and can be directed to specific areas of the plant. This method of application is particularly useful for plants with damaged roots or when the soil is very dry. These fertilizers should not be used on hot sunny days, however, as they may cause leaf scorch.

HOW MUCH FERTILIZER?

The easiest way to calculate exactly how much fertilizer each tree or shrub needs is to measure out to the 'drip line' (where the rain water drips off the branches). For most trees and shrubs, this will work out to be an area of between 1–3 sq.m (3-10 sq.ft). Then you simply multiply the recommended fertilizer rate by the number of meters (or feet) for each plant.

FEEDING CONTAINER-GROWN PLANTS

To promote healthy container plants, use proprietory pre-mixed soils that contain measured amounts of fertilizers. You can also use additional feeds as a top dressing, or apply foliar feed or fertilizer spikes, in the growing season when plants need a boost. Group containers together, so that you can feed them more quickly and easily.

WATERING

Like us, plants are principally composed of water and this needs replacing on a regular basis. To cut down on the amount of watering you have to do, you need to be able to time the quantities, and to deliver it in less time-consuming ways.

PLANTS MUST HAVE water, and applying it can be one of the most time-consuming tasks in the garden, especially if a watering can is the main method of delivery.

A plant can consist of as much as 90 per cent water, which is constantly being moved around within it. If the amount of water lost from the leaves exceeds that taken in by the roots, the plant will wilt.

Water is essential for a plant to live, because all of its basic functions and chemical processes need moisture, and without it, the plant will die. The moisture around the roots allows nutrients and minerals within the soil to be absorbed.

Within the plant, moisture keeps the cells firm and allows the movement of starches and sugars needed for growth. In the initial stages of growth, moisture triggers the swelling of seeds, and their germination, and seedlings, in particular, suffer badly in dry

conditions because they have no reserves on which to draw.

THE IMPORTANCE OF CLIMATE

The amount of watering you will need to do depends very much on the climate in which you live. Gardening against your natural climate, or trying to grow damp-loving plants in a dry climate or vice versa, will increase your

workload dramatically. Latitude, altitude, and distance from the sea all determine local climate. Even in a small garden, it is possible to create some particular 'microclimate' to suit certain plants—a pond for moisture-loving plant types, or a sheltered sunny spot for sun-lovers.

Much of the water provided by rainfall is lost through surface run-off and evaporation. Drought is a common problem, especially during summer. But a lack of rain at any time of the year can prove fatal, particularly for young or vulnerable plants.

TIMING THE WATERING

There are certain times in the development of any plant when its need for water it at its greatest. During seed germination and early seedling growth, it is important to maintain a constant level of moisture, or the process will stop. For fruiting plants

---

RAIN SHADOW

Any tall building will create a rain shadow area on the lee side of prevailing winds, in which the soil will be permanently dry; tall buildings and trees will also cast shade. These areas need to be planted with appropriate plants that thrive in low rainfall and light shade, if you are not to spend unnecessary time watering. Alternatively, grow your plants in open ground, so that they get the full benefit of the rain.

The diagram shows that no rain falls on the side of the house facing away from the prevailing wind. Rain shadows also cause problems on the leeward sides of walls and solid fences.

WATERING EQUIPMENT

You will find it useful to have a hose with a sprinkler or jet sprayer for easier watering, plus a watering can with a fine rose spray nozzle, for jobs such as watering young seedlings.

Hose

Jet sprayer

Watering can

Rotary sprinkler

and vegetables, extra water is needed at blossom time, fruit-set, and as the edible part develops. Too little water will lead to slow, stunted growth, and erratic watering will interrupt the plant's natural growth pattern.

If plants have to be watered, choosing the correct time of day can mean huge savings in the amount of water lost to evaporation from the soil's surface, and is time well spent. The best time to water is in the early morning or late evening, when the soil is cool and the atmosphere is relatively moist, allowing the water maximum time to soak in and be of most use to the plants. Watering in the heat of the day not only guarantees maximum evaporation, but also brings the danger of droplets on the leaves causing scorch. Set your seep hose or timed watering devices to water in the early morning or late at night, too.

HOW MUCH WATER?

Most plants have critical periods when a regular supply of water is very important for a key stage of their development. Peas, beans, tomatoes, and other vegetables where the fruit is eaten have two critical periods for water availability once they have established; when they flower (to aid pollination and fruit-set), and after the fruit has started to show obvious signs of swelling.

HOW OFTEN TO WATER?

This is the most difficult factor to assess, because every soil is different. When water is applied, always thoroughly soak the soil to a reasonable depth, to encourage the root system to follow the water downwards. It is worth looking at plants from a slightly different angle for a low-maintenance garden, and if at all possible, group plants together according to their

watering requirements. Those plants that seem to prefer dry conditions can be grown in the same area and will hardly ever need watering, while those that need more water can be grouped together and watering can be concentrated on that particular area.

As a rule, plants with deeper root systems are better equipped to cope with dry conditions, and plants that naturally grow in dry hot conditions, such as some grasses and silver-leaved plants, are those that often thrive with little or no watering. The shape and growth habit of some plants can also have an effect on the amount of water they can conserve. Herbaceous plants, shrubs, and conifers which have a 'dome-shaped', spreading habit and low, spreading branches covering the soil are very effective at conserving moisture in the soil, because their shoots and branches form a living mulch that shades the soil where plant roots are located. This will reduce evaporation from the soil and keep the roots cool.

ABOVE Raised beds and massed containers help minimize bending and make all kinds of chores, from weeding to watering, much easier to deal with.

WATERING GUIDE

Plant requirements	Water (litres/week)
Bedding plants	10–15
Clematis	10+
Fruit bush	13+
Hanging basket	7–14
Lawn	25+
Ornamental tree	16+
Vegetables	22+

Application rates from appliances

Appliance	litres/hour
Hose pipe 15m (45ft)	540–1000
Lawn sprinkler	300–650
Seep hose 30m (90ft)	60–120
Watering can (2gallons)	10

These figures are guides for summer periods when no rain has fallen.

WATER BEHAVIOUR

Water moves down through the soil in a 'moisture front', where the top layer of soil becomes fully wet before the water penetrates to the next layer. The best way to check the progress is to dig a hole with a trowel and check the colour of the soil.

When gardening time is really at a premium, some form of garden 'plumbing system' is an absolute must. They are relatively cheap to buy, easy to install, and can be turned on or off by a battery-powered timing device, which means that wired electricity is not essential.

Another advantage of this type of watering is that it will often work on a system that takes advantage of low pressure. Water is only released from the pipes when they are full, so that even if it takes 30 minutes or more before the water starts to reach the plants, the plants will still be watered, and the water will continue to drain out of the pipes even after the supply is turned off. Seep hoses and drip nozzles allow the water to penetrate the soil in

AUTOMATIC WATERING

There are various automatic watering systems that will save watering by hand. They consist of either seep hoses (above), which are hoses with perforations for water to seep out, or drip-feed systems (left), consisting of pipes with nozzles at intervals through which the water emerges. A soil moisture detector can be fitted to the latter, which overrides the automatic system if the ground is damp enough.

WATER PENETRATION WITH A SEEP HOSE

In the diagram below, you can see that the plant's roots spread out as far as its canopy of leaves. The seep hose system laid on the surface of the soil has a series of small holes through which water emerges over the plant's root area, enabling the water to be delivered to where it is most needed.

RIGHT The small holes of the seep hose are organized so that they occur only over the plant's rooting surface.

a 'cone' shape so that most of the water is delivered to the point where it can do the most good. For individual plants that are widely spaced, a submerged plant pot or plastic bottle will act as a reservoir to hold the water and release it gradually. This will aid efficient watering (which saves time because it is not necessary to water so often), and encourage the plants to form a deep root system, which helps them cope better with dry periods.

For watering a lawn, far better results can be achieved with a hose pipe than a sprinkler, which looks very dramatic, but is not really all that efficient. Lay the end of the pipe in an area of the lawn, with the water running from it in a trickle that is barely visible, and leave it in one position for about half an hour before moving the end of the pipe to a different point.

USING MULCHES

As well as acting to suppress weeds, mulches can be used to conserve moisture within the soil by restricting evaporation. This means that more water is available to the plant for longer, allowing it to withstand short periods of drought without the need for extra water to be applied.

For sheet mulches, such as plastic, make sure that the area around the base of the plant is fractionally lower than the surrounding soil, so that any water falling onto the mulch has to drain away by passing close to the plants, giving them the chance to take up the water as it passes. A covering of black plastic is the most efficient form of mulch, and although alone it is not much to look at, it can be covered with 5cm (2in) of bark or gravel. (For more information on mulches, see pages 100-101.)

ABOVE Gravel makes a useful moisture-retaining mulch, and is well worth using in hot, dry climates to help conserve water.

WATERING CONTAINERS

Plants in containers lose water very rapidly through evaporation. Terracotta pots especially are notoriously poor at retaining moisture. Hanging baskets, with their small amount of soil and large area exposed to the elements, are very greedy for water and may well need watering once a day in hot weather.

A major difficulty with growing plants in containers is keeping the plants supplied with water, especially when using loamless soils, as these are very difficult to re-wet after drying out.

To overcome this, add granules of polymer to the compost. When wetted, these granules swell to form a moisture-retaining gel that can hold vast amounts of water. The water is gradually released into the soil.

Containers also benefit from having the surface covered with pebbles and from standing close together on a pebble surface, as this reduces evaporation. To keep plants moist, stand the container on a bed of pebbles in a tray of water.

USING A GRAVEL BASE
If you go away for a few days, place your containers on gravel-filled trays, filled with water. These will feed the pots with a regular supply of water without waterlogging the roots.

PENETRATING THE SOIL
Use a pencil or stick to make five holes round the edge of the pot. These provide water channels when the plant is watered.

REVIVING A WILTED PLANT
If a plant has started to dry out, plunge the whole pot into a bucket of water and leave until air bubbles stop rising.

WATERING A HANGING BASKET
High baskets can be more easily watered by attaching a cane to the hosepipe with ties to make a rigid spout.

SUPPRESSING WEEDS

Of all the tasks that consume the gardener's time, weeding is probably the most laborious and persistently recurring. Any low-maintenance garden must offer long-term solutions to cutting down on weeding, while still retaining its aesthetic appeal.

GRAVEL AS MULCH

This small dry border has been given a weed-suppressing mulch of black plastic, covered with gravel to improve its aesthetic appeal. Mulching has a double benefit. It cuts down on maintenance by suppressing weeds and preserves what little moisture there is in the soil.

Prevention is the most effective method of weed control—stop light reaching the soil surface and the weed problem will be practically solved. The solution also needs to look attractive, and while laying concrete will control the weeds, it will impose great limitations on any form of gardening. Two much more attractive (and flexible) alternatives are mulches or ground-cover plants (see pages 32-33) to cover the soil, or a combination of the two. Using ground cover to suppress weeds is only effective if the soil is completely cleared of perennial weeds before planting.

The idea of mulching is to cover the soil and block out the light to prevent weeds germinating using organic or inorganic substances (see opposite). Organic mulches, such as bark, must be applied as a 10cm (4in) thick layer and will need topping up once a year as they break down and decompose.

MULCHING AROUND TREES AND SHRUBS

There are various areas of the garden in which black plastic mulch (covered with bark chippings or gravel for aesthetic effect) are most valuable. One in particular is around the base of young trees or plants while you are waiting for the plants to grow and do their own work in suppressing weeds as their canopy covers the soil and deprives weed seed of light.

1 Clear the soil first, and remove any perennial weeds. Then cut a large square of black plastic (about 60cm/24in square) and cut it to the centre on one side. Lay it around the base of the tree as shown.

2 Cut crosses in the black plastic where you wish to insert any new ground-covering plants. Start to insert the plants through the crosses in the black plastic, and water well.

3 Finally, spread bark chippings or gravel over the black plastic to disguise it. This will also have the effect of keeping the plastic in place.

WEED-SUPPRESSING MULCHES

Types of mulch	When to apply/reapply	Where to use
 **Fibre fleece** A lightweight inorganic mulch that helps to raise soil temperatures.	Any time of year to weed-free soil, preferably before planting. Will last for about seven years if protected from sunlight.	Ideal for long-term ornamental beds, where organic mulch or pebbles are laid on top.
 **Woven black plastic** A heavy-duty inorganic mulch, it is the most effective form for suppressing perennial weeds	Any time of year, preferably before planting starts as it will smother existing weeds. Will last about 15 years if protected from sunlight.	Good for long-term plantings, such as ornamental shrub beds, where organic mulch or pebbles are laid on top. Works well in combination with ground-cover plants.
 **Grit/gravel** An inorganic mulch, useful for plants that require free drainage. Plants self-seed in it if it is not used over plastic sheets.	Any time of year to weed-free soil. Will gradually work into the soil, so needs topping up every five years. Apply before or after planting, at a depth of 7-10cm (3-4in).	Good for long-term plantings. Works well in combination with plastic or fleece to create a more aesthetically pleasing surface
 **Pebbles** Inorganic mulch; very decorative when colours and sizes are varied and mixed with gravel. Useful for absorbing the ambient heat and conserving the soil's moisture.	Any time of the year to weed-free soil, before or after planting. Will last for many years. Most effective used in conjunction with black plastic or matting on soil surface.	Best choice for long-term mulching. Very good for drought-tolerant plants and Oriental-style gardens.
 **Wood chippings** Organic mulch that looks very attractive, especially against greenery. An effective weed suppressor. If you have a small electric chipper, you can shred your own prunings.	In autumn or early spring before weeds emerge. Will gradually work into the soil, so needs topping up every second year. Apply before or after planting, at a depth of 7-10cm (3-4in).	Looks best when used with conifers and evergreens. Encourages biological activity within the soil and may improve fertility, although some nitrogen deficiency may occur soon after application.
Cacao fibre Also called cocoa shells, this organic mulch is relatively expensive but good for small city borders, for example. However, do not use where domestic animals may dig it up.	In autumn or early spring before weeds emerge. Top up every second year. Easy to apply before or after planting, at a depth of 7-10cm (3-4in).	Very attractive, especially when used with heathers or evergreens. Encourages biological activity within the soil and may also improve its fertility.

MAINTAINING LAWNS

Lawns can be highly demanding in terms of maintenance, but by employing a few useful shortcuts you can save yourself a great deal of energy and effort and dramatically reduce the number of hours spent on mowing and trimming.

WHATEVER KIND OF lawn you have, if you want it to look green and healthy year-round, you will need to pay some attention to maintenance, apart from regular mowing. Lawn grasses have vigorous roots which tend to mat together, so once a year you need to aerate the root area by spiking the soil—by hiring a mechanical scarifier for large lawns, or simply by jabbing it at regular intervals with a garden fork for a small one. Your lawn will also need feeding to replace the nitrogen lost when grass clippings are removed. Special lawn preparations can be bought and should be applied according to manufacturer's directions.

Make sure that any annual weeds are removed regularly; mowing will help prevent them germinating. Broad-leaved weeds can be removed using selective weedkillers, but if you want a low-maintenance lawn you may have to put up with a certain amount of weediness.

It is worth remembering that mowing a lawn actually stimulates growth, and the more frequently it's cut, the faster it will grow. Leaving the grass slightly longer and only cutting it once each week to about 2-3cm (1in) above the soil will help to slow down growth.

Wildflower meadows are sometimes offered as an alternative to a formal lawn, but these are not low-maintenance if a wide range of species are to be kept. The flowering grasses can also make life very unpleasant for gardeners who suffer from hay fever.

LAYING A LAWN

This is generally not a good idea for low-maintenance gardeners who would be better off opting for a different kind of surface. If you do want a lawn, bear in mind that the surface must be well prepared and absolutely even or your work will double. The easiest method, although not the cheapest, is to buy ready prepared turf that comes in small rolls, like a carpet.

MODIFYING A LAWN

Plan the layout of beds and borders to fit the requirements of the mower. Make it easier by changing the shape

LEFT AND ABOVE

If you have a lawn, ensure that the surrounds are lower than the lawn, so that you can mow over them easily. You can adopt the same system with a stepping stone path to save wear and tear on the lawn, set 2cm (1in) below the lawn surface level.

EASY-CARE ALTERNATIVES

There are some situations where it may not be desirable or necessary to have a lawn. Maybe there is just too much work involved, or the site may be unsuitable if the garden is too shady or too wet, particularly in cities, where it may be surrounded by taller buildings. It takes two or three times longer to maintain a poor lawn than a healthy one on a good site. It can be pleasantly surprising just how many options are available as an alternative to a patch of grass. Plants such as chamomile are suitable for some areas, and will give a lawn-like appearance while requiring little cutting.

Low-growing plants used as ground cover can look more attractive than grass, especially in dry soils and shaded areas where grass is struggling. Selecting the right type of plant will make it possible to have colour and interest from foliage fruits and flowers—with no mowing.

LEFT A chamomile lawn is not only maintenance-free, it is also aromatic and very springy under foot, retaining its green texture throughout the year.

PLANTS FOR A NON-GRASS LAWN

Buttonweed (*Leptinella atrata*)
Chamomile (*Chamaemelum nobile*)
Chamomile 'Treneague' (*Chamaemelum nobile* 'Treneague')
Convolvulus (*Dichondra micrantha*)
Corsican mint (*Mentha requienii*)
Pennyroyal (*Mentha pulegium*)
Wild thyme (*Thymus serpyllum*)

and dimensions to speed up maintenance. Square or rectangular lawns with corners can take up to three times longer to cut than those with curves. Where beds are cut into the lawn, make any grass pathways between flower beds fit the dimensions of the mower's cutting width. For instance, if the mower has a cutting width of 45cm (18in), make pathways in width multiples of this, so that a 90cm (3ft) pathway can be cut in two passes.

Having to go back and cut a narrow 10cm (4in) strip takes as long as cutting another 45cm (18in) strip and is awkward. Tasks like trimming or recutting lawn edges can be eliminated by creating a 'mowing strip' of flat bricks or paving stones around the edge of the lawn. This strip can also act as a guide for the height of cut, if it is set even with the lawn's surface, and it provides a firm edge for the mower's wheels (or rim if it is a hover-type mower), reducing the

chances of the lawn edge being 'scalped' if the wheels run onto the border.

REPAIRING LAWNS

If areas of the lawn become worn, you can remove the turf in squares, like carpet tiles, and relay them, using a piece of untrodden turf to replace the worn one. Cut around the square with a half-moon edger and slide a spade under the turf, about 7.5cm (3in) down, to remove it. Relay it immediately.

WATERING A LAWN

Most well-kept lawns will only require watering for about two to three months in an average year. However, sometimes there are dry periods when soil water reserves are not sufficient.

The usual signs of water stress are grass blades taking on a dull sheen, often with a bluish tint, and footprints that are easy to see as the grass is limp and does not spring

back into position. The way in which water is applied is more important than the quantity of water: always ensure the lawn is given a good soaking, since frequent, light applications in dry weather encourages shallow rooting and makes the grass more vulnerable. Regular lawn watering is easier with a sprinkler, which needs to be moved to cover large areas.

PROPAGATING

Some plants are extremely easy to grow and it is well worth your while increasing some of your own stocks of plants as it is far less expensive than buying them new from a nursery.

Plant propagation often comes across as fiddly and time-consuming—but, in fact you can easily increase plant numbers without the need for complicated techniques or special facilities.

You will need some basic equipment for propagating, including seed trays and/or small pots, appropriate sowing and cuttings soil, and a few plastic bags (or plastic bottles) to cover trays and pots while seeds germinate and cuttings take root. If you grow seeds in biodegradable pots, you can simply insert the pot into a larger pot when the seedling or cutting has reached an appropriate size, saving time and effort, and also avoiding disturbing delicate roots.

SOWING SEEDS

The seeds of many hardy plants, including annuals, herbaceous perennials, trees, and shrubs, are quite

LEFT These young chamomile plants have been grown from seed. They are relatively easy to germinate and can be transplanted at this size to create a chamomile lawn — an easy alternative to grass lawns (see pages 36-37).

happy to be sown in the open garden rather than in a heated propagator. The only difference is likely to be that germination will take slightly longer. The seeds can still be sown into small pots, but by plunging the pots into the border soil up to rim-level, then the soil will be kept moist by the surrounding earth, reducing the need for watering. A two-litre plastic drinks bottle with the cap and base removed can be placed over the pot to act as a cloche or mini-greenhouse to provide protection and extra warmth.

TAKING CUTTINGS

For some plants, taking cuttings can be even easier than growing them from seed. All you need is a small area of border soil and some dormant, one-year-old twigs taken from deciduous plants. Cut the stems into 15cm (6in) lengths and insert them right-way up, up to two-thirds of their length into the soil. Over the next year, these cuttings

will produce roots and shoots, and the following winter, the new plants are ready for moving to a permanent site.

Softwood or semi-ripe cuttings can be inserted into small pots of soil, with the pot plunged into the border soil up to rim level. This will keep the soil moist and cool, as the surrounding soil provides moisture and acts as an insulator, which reduces the need for

GROWING FROM SEED
Seed sowing is not time-consuming if you plant in small containers in sowing soil and cover with plastic to conserve moisture.

SUCCESSFUL CUTTINGS
Softwood cuttings taken in early summer will reliably create new rooted plants, but take more cuttings than needed to allow for failures.

watering. A plastic drinks bottle with the cap and base removed can be placed over the pot, and used as a cloche or mini-greenhouse to provide protection, extra warmth, and help stop them from drying out. This type of propagation works better if the cuttings are placed in a shaded part of the garden so that they are not in direct sunlight during the heat of the day. Some plants strike remarkably easily from softwood cuttings. Among them are box (*Buxus sempervirens*), rosemary (*Rosmarinus officinalis*), and lavender (*Lavandula* sp.).

DIVIDING PLANTS

Most herbaceous perennials and some shrubs can be increased in numbers just by lifting them out of the ground and splitting them into smaller clumps before replanting them. Although this is often considered a winter job, most plants can be divided from late autumn through to early spring and some plants such as flag iris (*Iris germanica*) are divided in the summer immediately after they have finished flowering.

Dig up the plant and wash it thoroughly to remove as much soil as possible. Washing will reduce the amount of wear and damage on any knives and secateurs being used.

With tough, herbaceous subjects, the fibrous-rooted clump can be divided by easing the roots apart with two forks placed back to back in the centre of the clump. The forks are pulled together forcing the tines apart, splitting the clump.

Each of the severed portions of plant should have some roots and at least one growth bud present in order to produce a new plant. Any dead or diseased sections of these clumps should be discarded before replanting.

Dig a planting hole large enough to accommodate the plant's root system, and replant the new divisions.

Most plants will flower within a year of being divided, and using division to thin out plant growth reduces overcrowding, which helps to eliminate pests and diseases. To increase bulbs, you can simply remove any offsets (small bulbs attached to the parent bulb) and replant them, at twice their own depth. It will take more than a couple of years, however, before they reach a sufficient size to flower.

DIVIDING SMALL PERENNIALS

Small perennials can be divided and cut with a garden knife. Ensure that each divided portion of root bears a growing tip.

DIVIDING LARGE PERENNIALS

More densely rooted perennials will need to be pulled apart. Use two forks, back to back, to do so.

LOW-MAINTENANCE PROPAGATING

The simplest way to propagate a shrub with fairly pliable branches that bend down to soil level is to layer them. Select a young flexible shoot, bend it down to the soil's surface, and mark a point some distance along the stem where it reaches this spot on the soil. Create a small planting hole and fill with cuttings soil. Then make a cut on the underside of the shoot at the appropriate point, twist open the cut to make sure a large area of cut surface is exposed, and then bend down the shoot so that the cut is in contact with the soil. Cover over with soil, and weight the branch if necessary with a stone. After six months or so, the cut part of the shoot will have developed small roots. Sever this portion from the parent plant and repot.

1 Trim off sideshoots from the chosen shoot, and cut the underside of the branch a third of the way through, without cutting it right off.

2 Twist the cut to allow maximum contact with the soil, push it down into the prepared soil, and cover. Weight with a stone.

PRUNING

The bugbear of many gardeners, pruning is only a problem if your goal is to produce gold-medal-winning displays of flowers or fruit. You can simplify the task and cut down on time and worry if you follow a few simple rules.

THE IDEA OF pruning usually worries new gardeners but there are two golden rules: first, that shrubs will need to be pruned to keep them compact yet open in shape, and second, that pruning is best carried out directly after flowering. Much of the mystery attached to pruning is because it is easy, in ignorance, to prune off the stems that bear the next season's flowers, but not if you apply the second golden rule!

Many ornamental plants are shaped using a combination of cutting and training, with some being very time-consuming indeed. Roses are pruned to increase the size and number of blooms, while hedge trimming is used to produce a particular type of dense,

compact growth. Some plants can be left alone and only pruned when they begin to encroach over a path or begin to smother a neighbouring plant. Although the plants concerned may not produce quite so many flowers as those that are pruned regularly, they perform well enough to satisfy most gardeners and are ideal where maintenance is to be kept to a minimum.

With a little research before you buy, it is also possible to choose plants that need little or no pruning, grow and flower well, look good, and provide attraction for one or more seasons. They should not be varieties that grow quickly or achieve great height or width: among the best are slow-

growing evergreens such as *Skimmia japonica*, *Viburnum davidii* and many of the hebes, for example. Use a mixture of evergreen and deciduous shrubs and small trees to provide a framework within the garden for seasonal plants such as bulbs and herbaceous perennials. If your plants do require pruning, this should be done on a regular basis, with a clear idea in mind of what you want to achieve.

LOW-MAINTENANCE METHODS
Shrubs such as lilac and magnolia very rarely need pruning, and apart from removing old flower heads or the occasional split or damaged branch, plants like these can be left more or less to their own devices.

REASONS TO PRUNE

There are five main reasons to prune: to maintain plant health; to obtain a balance between growth and flowering; to train the plant; to restrict growth, and to improve the quality of fruit or flowers. You can eradicate pests and diseases by pruning out dead, diseased and damaged parts, but it is far more effective to prune as a preventative measure to maintain plant health. Pruning a young plant forms the framework of sturdy, evenly spaced branches that will eventually produce flowers and fruit. By pruning out older shoots and diverting energy into the development of fruit and buds, you will also encourage an older plant to flower or fruit more profusely.

HEALTH

This shoot has died back due to bad pruning and must be cut back as far as healthy wood.

TRAINING

Fruit tree stems are trained horizontally to encourage flowers and fruits to form.

QUALITY

Removing dead flowers is vital to prevent seed formation and encourage more flowers to form.

RENOVATING PLANTS

Neglected shrubs often respond to severe pruning and produce healthy new growth from the base of the plant.

To do this, cut the shrubs down to about 45cm (18in) in spring, just before growth starts. The following spring, shape any vigorous new growth to create a more balanced shape.

For less drastic action, reshape the plant by cutting the oldest stems down to ground level. This will give the remaining branches more air, thus encouraging healthier growth.

ABOVE Cut down roughly one third of the plant's branches, choosing the oldest wood, down to the base in spring.

Others, such as the autumn-flowering clematis, need pruning only once each year, usually in February, when all of the shoots are cut back to 30–45cm (12–18in) above ground level.

Using secateurs and shears can take longer than pruning with a saw or loppers. Trimming plants with secateurs or shears stimulates masses of new growth, which needs trimming again a few weeks later. A more rapid system for deciduous shrubs (which is also more beneficial to the plants) is to take out the oldest shoots entirely by cutting them down to ground level with a saw or loppers, leaving the young, strong, healthy shoots completely untouched. Removing one-third of all the shoots completely each year still allows the shrub to flower well and look good. By the fourth year of pruning, all of the original shoots will have been replaced, although the rotation can still be continued, removing the three-year-old wood. This is important as the older growth is most susceptible to attack by pests and diseases, especially where old, flaking bark provides perfect sites for fungal spores and insect eggs to overwinter.

Unless you spend a large amount of time gardening, it is difficult to build up a knowledge of plants—how they grow and what they need to keep growing well. However, when it comes to pruning shrubs, there are short cuts. Most will only flower once on the same piece of wood, so after a shoot has borne flowers, it might as well be removed. As a rule, shrubs benefit from being pruned at the correct time—the correct time for most being immediately after flowering. Doing this while the dead flowers are still on the plant will indicate which shoots should be removed. This then leaves a whole year for new growth to form and produce flowers, and ensures that plants only need to be pruned once a year.

The main exception to this rule are shrubs such as *Buddleja davidii*, which flower in early autumn, and are pruned in spring—if they are pruned immediately after flowering, the new shoots may be damaged by winter frosts.

VARIEGATED PLANTS

These need pruning to remove any growths where the leaves are completely green, rather than having any gold or silver markings. The plain growth is more vigorous, and if left, these shoots will take control and the attractive variegated leaves will gradually disappear. Prune the plants when they are in full leaf so you can identify the right shoots.

RIGHT Removing a non-variegated shoot from a shrub.

WHEN TO PRUNE

Shrubs can be divided into four basic pruning groups. Plants belonging to Group 1 require very little or no pruning (e.g. *Amelanchier, Buddleja globosa, Camellia, Elaeagnus pungens, Hamamelis, Magnolia stellata, Viburnum tomentosum*); Those that belong to Group 2 flower on the current season's growth and should be pruned in spring (e.g. *Buddleja davidii, Euonymus europaeus* cvs, *Forsythia, Fuchsia magellanica, Hibiscus, Hydrangea, Lavandula, Spiraea japonica*). Plants in Group 3 flower on the previous season's growth and should be pruned in summer after flowering (e.g. *Buddleja alternifolia, Chaenomeles, Deutzia, Exochorda, Rhododendron liteum, Ribes sanguineum*). Plants belonging to Group 4 have a suckering habit or coloured stems (e.g. *Berberis, Corylus, Fuchsia, Mahonia aquifolium, Rosa rugosa, Sarcococca*).

REDUCING CHORES

*No garden is entirely maintenance-free and there are some chores that cannot
be avoided. However, there are ways to cut down on these and to ensure that they are
done as efficiently as possible.*

ONCE YOU HAVE opted for low-maintenance surfaces, like paving, decking or gravel, you still have to pay them some attention, although they require a lot less care than a growing medium like a lawn. Leaves from surrounding deciduous trees will drop in autumn and you will be faced with the task of clearing them up. For a small urban patio, you might invest in an outdoor vacuum cleaner but even if you do, it is worth keeping the leaves, bagging them up in garden plastic sacks, sticking them with a fork to puncture them and then storing them in an out-of-the-way corner for a few seasons to eventually return to the garden as leaf mulch. Make sure the crowns of various perennials and

ABOVE If you have perennial weeds, the easiest option (although not the most ecologically friendly) is to spray them with a contact weedkiller, such as glyphosate, once a year, following the manufacturer's directions.

shrubs are kept as leaf-free as possible to prevent spreading disease and to ensure that plants are not smothered.

CLEARING WEEDS

The simplest way to deal with weeds is to remove them physically, either by pulling or digging them out, or if they are small, hoeing them off at soil level.

To get rid of weeds that grow up between cracks in paving, you may need to use a contact weedkiller. Should you want a more ecologically friendly solution, try filling the spaces with low-growing alpine plants. Not only will they compete with the weeds and block out the light reaching them, but they will also provide colour, interest and even aroma, if you choose varieties of plants such as thyme, which will tolerate being trodden on now and again, and will release their aromatic oils into the air whenever it happens.

LEFT Raking up leaves in autumn is one task that you cannot easily avoid. For small gardens, an outdoor vacuum cleaner saves much back-breaking work.

TYING IN CLIMBERS AND WALL SHRUBS

To reduce the amount of time spent tying plants in place, it is important to consider first what climbers you are buying, what kind of support you need and how the plant is to be trained on it. Remember that the more vigorous the

ABOVE If you are growing climbers that are not self-supporting, you will need to tie them in once or twice a year.

Divide pond plants every two to three years to prevent them from overcrowding the pond.

Softwood planks (decking or fences) need an annual coat of preservative to stay rot-free.

In cold climates, wrap pots of plants that are not frost-hardy with bubble wrap or sacking.

plants involved, the more tying and training will be required. Use the plant's own tendencies to cut down on the work. Climbers will grow towards sunlight, and this characteristic can be used to help support the plant with a minimum of tying.

MAINTAINING PONDS

Ponds will need occasional clearing of oxygenating plants, which tend to grow quite rapidly. Simply pull out one-third of their mass each autumn. Once every couple of years, divide the plants that are outgrowing their pots, and give

away the unwanted roots to new pond owners. In spring, if you keep fish, you may need to give the pond a dose of pond salts to maintain a healthy balance for the fish. Once every four years or so, you may need to do a complete clean out of the pond base to remove fallen leaves (unless you net the pond in autumn to save yourself this task).

KEEPING HARD SURFACES TIDY

As well as sweeping patios and paved surfaces, you will need to pay attention to fencing and decking. Hardwoods need an annual scrub with a stiff brush and a coat

of algaecide in wet climates, while softwoods will need an annual coat of preservative. Wood stains will also need renewing every couple of years.

OVERWINTERING

Tender plants will need putting down for the winter. Container grown tender plants can have their pots bubble-wrapped or sacking can be tied around them. Tender perennials can have their crowns protected (with their own leaves, if large, or with hessian). Move really tender plants into a greenhouse or indoors for winter (see below).

MOVING HEAVY CONTAINERS

Although containers are a great boon to gardeners, offering the opportunity to plant in otherwise difficult areas and to change the focus of the planting by moving them into prominent positions when in flower, they can be quite difficult to move around.

There are a few ways to do this more easily. One of them is to push the container onto a flat piece of board, and then insert dowelling rods under the board, so that you can roll the container along. You could also keep a container on a piece of board with castors, if frequent movement is likely.

With another person's help, shift the container onto a piece of heavy-duty plastic or sacking and then drag the cloth (above) or carefully roll a container on the edge of its base (right).

EASIER HEDGES

Looking after hedges is probably the most time-consuming element in the garden, after lawn care. Choosing appropriate plants is one solution to cutting down on hedge care, because slow-growing evergreens or informal flowering hedges create less work.

REGARDLESS OF WHICH style of gardening you are interested in, there will always be an element of routine. There are always jobs that need to be done, often several times a year. Many of these jobs can be tedious, but the aim of the low-maintenance approach to gardening is to reduce these routine tasks to a bare minimum.

LOOKING AFTER HEDGES

The plaintive cry when the subject of hedges is raised is that although they are undoubtedly much more attractive to look at than panel fences, they are far more labour-intensive to maintain. But are they? A hedge is actually only as labour-intensive as the gardener wants it to be. By choosing the right plant for the situation, you can have total control of the amount of maintenance it will need—and even a panel fence needs treating with preservative once a year.

LEFT Informal hedges need relatively little care and attention to keep them looking good but they should be trimmed two or three times a year.

Regardless of which plants are to be used, there are two basic types of hedge: formal hedges, which require regular clipping or trimming to control growth and maintain the desired shape (up to eight times each year), and informal hedges, which are given only a bare minimum of pruning to encourage the individual plants to flower and prevent them from becoming overgrown and untidy.

The informal hedge can be very attractive, and there is far less work involved—usually only one cut a year. How and when to prune depends mainly upon when the hedge flowers, but as a general rule, this type of hedge should be pruned immediately after flowering, to remove those branches that have just borne flowers.

Often the same plants can be used for both formal or informal hedges, but there can be some drawbacks with certain species. For example, both laurel and privet make very good formal hedges, and quite presentable informal hedges. However, when grown as informal hedges, both produce

PRUNING HEDGES

PLANT	EVERGREEN/DECIDUOUS	WHEN TO PRUNE
Berberis darwinii (barberry)	E	1 x after flowering
Berberis thunbergii	D	1 x after flowering
Cotoneaster lacteus	E	1 x after fruiting
Crataegus monogyna (hawthorn)	D	1 x winter
Escallonia	E	1 x after flowering
Forsythia x intermedia	D	1 x after flowering
Fuchsia magellanica	D	1 x spring remove old stems
Garrya elliptica (tassel bush)	E	1 x after flowering
Ilex aquifolium (holly)	E	1 x late-summer
Lavandula (lavender)	E	1 x after flowering
Pyracantha (firethorn)	E	1 x after fruiting
Rosa rugosa (rose)	D	1 x spring remove oldest shoots
Viburnum tinus	E	1 x after flowering

MIXED HEDGE BEFORE PRUNING

Mixed shrubs in a hedge will grow at different rates. Prune once a year when the hedge starts to look untidy.

MIXED HEDGE AFTER PRUNING

Cut back any very vigorous plants, removing any long, struggling stems. Lightly clip the remaining stems.

(broadleaf) *Ilex aquifolium* (holly) and *Prunus laurocerasus* (laurel).

NO-CUT PRUNING

One alternative to frequent hedge trimming is to try and slow down the growth rate of the plants which make up the hedge. There are a number of growth regulators that can be used to slow down the growth of many types of hedge plant (ask for advice from your local nursery or garden specialist). These regulators can be sprayed onto the hedge in the spring within a few days of clipping to slow down the new growth as it develops. Usually only one application is required, and there is no further need to clip the hedge again.

strongly perfumed flowers with an aroma that many gardeners find unpleasant. Indeed, some gardeners find that the perfume of laurel flowers causes headaches when they are working nearby.

Some evergreens, such as box and yew, make good hedges because they need much less frequent trimming than the more commonly grown privet (which will need cutting at least four times during the growing season). Until

REMOVING SHOOTS

Prune back broad-leaved evergreen hedges by removing the tips of growing shoots with secateurs.

they reach the required height, however, you will need to back them with a simple wire fence. A deciduous hedge that is also relatively slow growing is hornbeam, which needs only two cuts a year—although it will shed leaves in autumn that then have to be swept up.

HOW TO PRUNE

Usually, hand-operated or electrically powered shears are used for clipping hedges. However, this is difficult for broadleaved evergreen plants with larger leaves, such as laurel (*Prunus laurocerasus*), as pruning with shears will mutilate many larger leaves and spoil the overall effect of the hedge until new growth has developed. Leaves that are cut in half develop a brown line where the cells have been damaged and these 'half-leaves' slowly turn yellow and die. This means that secateurs should be used with this type of plant, which, unfortunately, can take up to 20 times longer than using shears. Plants unsuitable for trimming with shears or hedgecutters include *Elaeagnus* x *ebbingei* (elaeagnus), *Griselinia littoralis*

USING A POWER HEDGE TRIMMER

These are ideal for trimming a long hedge, and far less time-consuming. If you don't own a power trimmer, you can easily hire one for the day and get the job done quickly. Electric trimmers are better than petrol-powered models, as they are lighter, less noisy, and don't produce fumes. When using a mechanical trimmer, always keep the blade parallel to the surface of the hedge.

ABOVE Wearing gloves and goggles, cut the hedge in a broad, sweeping action, working from the bottom upwards.

PESTS AND DISEASES

No gardens are pest- and disease-free, although some plants are more resistant than others. Healthy plants generally succumb less readily to attacks, and working with nature is an obvious way to cut down on the work involved.

LOW-MAINTENANCE SHOULD not equal neglect. A little care and attention can save hours of pruning and spraying. Clearing up old plant debris at the end of the growing season not only makes the garden look tidier, it reduces the number of sites where pests and diseases can overwinter before infecting the new, sappy growth in spring. Much of this material can be composted (the heat generated as the plant debris rots kills off harmful pests and diseases), although with certain pests, such as eelworms, or diseases like clubroot, the plants should be burned or dumped as these organisms may survive the heat of composting.

Some plants seem to have a natural resistance, or tolerance, to common pests and diseases, and selecting these for the garden can greatly reduce the amount of maintenance necessary. To use roses as an example, 'Peace' and 'Queen Elizabeth' are both partly resistant to rose mildew. 'Super Star' and 'Woburn Abbey', on the other hand, require spraying with a fungicide

ABOVE Well-fed and watered plants have a far greater resistance to disease, so ensure that yours are not neglected (see pages 94-9)

at three-week intervals from April until September to keep it at bay.

One of the best means of pest control in a low-maintenance garden is a bird feeder. By putting out a few select seeds and nuts to entice birds into the garden it is possible encourage them to forage for more food, such as aphids, caterpillars, and slugs. If chemicals are to be used, it is important to spray as soon as a pest or disease is spotted. By eradicating the problem before it can become established, it is possible to keep the amount of time spent spraying to a minimum.

Barriers, such as gravel mulches, may be used to prevent a pest from feeding, or break the life-cycle so that pest numbers decline.

GOOD COMPANIONS

Certain plants can be grown together as companions to protect one another from infestation by pest and disease. These plants tend to work in one of two ways. One way that they are effective is that they may contain or produce chemicals with an aroma or taste that repels pests or diseases, discouraging them from invading certain areas or plants. Alternatively, they can act as host plants or bait, attracting pests and diseases and drawing them away from important crop plants.

Plant	Companion plants
Apples	Wallflower
Broad Beans	Carrot and Celery
Cabbage	Beetroot and Chard
Lettuce	Carrots and Radish
Potato	Nasturtium and Tagetes
Raspberry	Marigold
Strawberry	Borage and Onions
Tomato	Basil and Carrot
Rose	Chives and Garlic
Sunflower	Cucumber and Corn

COMMON PESTS AND DISEASES

Aphids: Dense colonies of small green or black insects that suck sap from plants, including trees, shrubs, climbers, vegetables, and fruit, often causing distorted shoots and leaves.
Control Spray as soon as the first aphids are seen in late spring.

Earwigs Small brown insects up to 2.5cm (1in) long, with a pincer-like gripper on the tail. Feeding causes small circular notches or holes in leaves and flowers.
Control Use traps of straw-filled pots to catch adult insects, or spray badly affected plants with malathion. Some damage may be acceptable as earwigs also eat quite a number of aphids.

Slugs & snails Both usually feed at night, year-round on any plant they can reach.
Control Apply sharp mulches of gravel or soot around the plants as a barrier, use slug traps, or apply aluminium sulphate or slug pellets in the spring as the eggs hatch.

Scale insects These look like small brown blisters on stems and leaves. They suck the sap, causing stunted growth and yellow leaves.
Control Place a layer of barrier

glue around the stems of plants to stop the larval stage from moving onto the plant, or apply insecticide sprays in late spring and early summer.

Vine weevils These are white, legless grubs with a black or brown head, usually curled into a 'C' shape. They eat the roots of plants, causing wilt or total collapse.
Control Treat the soil around the plants with parasitic nematodes that kill the pest or, for container-grown plants, use soil containing the insecticide Imidacloprid.

Stem and bulb eelworm These minute pests live and feed inside the plant, causing weak, stunted growth, dead brown margins to leaves, and stems that thicken and rot.
Control Remove and burn infected plants.

Downy mildew A fungus causing yellow leaves, with white patches on the lower surface. Badly affected plants often die slowly in the autumn.
Control Prune to avoid overcrowding, use resistant cultivars, or spray with mancozeb as soon as the disease is spotted.

Powdery mildew This parasitic fungal disease invades the softer tissues inside the leaf causing white, floury patches on the leaves, distorted shoots, and premature leaf fall.
Control Prune out infected stems in autumn to prevent the fungus from overwintering, and spray with an appropriate fungicide at the first signs of infection.

Fireblight A bacterial disease that attacks the soft tissue of members of the rose family. Leaves wilt and turn brown, shoots die back, and plants eventually die.
Control Remove and burn any plants with the symptoms.

Coral spot This fungus invades both dead wood and live plant tissue, causing shoots to wilt in summer. In autumn, dead branches will be covered in small coral-pink spots.
Control Prune during summer when there are no fungal spores being released into the air, and burn infected material as quickly as possible.

Mosaic virus This very simple organism lives inside the plant and results in yellow, twisted leaves, poor weak growth, stunted shoots, and

misshapen flowers.
Control All infected plants should be removed and burned immediately.

Gray mold (Botrytis) This fungus infects flowers, leaves, and stems, causing yellow leaves, stem-rot at ground level, and the plant to become covered with a gray, felt-like mold.
Control Prune out any infected stems in the autumn to prevent the fungus from overwintering and spray with an appropriate fungicide at the first signs of infection.

Silver leaf This fungus enters through pruning wounds or damaged bark. Branches die back until the whole plant dies. The leaves of infected plants take on a silvery sheen.
Control Prune out infected branches and burn.

Damping-off This fungus will invade and kill infected plants. Seedlings keel over, rot, and die soon after germination or fail to emerge at all.
Control Use sterilized soil and containers when raising young plants, and use seed which has been treated with an appropriate fungicide.

Scale insect

Powdery mildew

Silver leaf

Coral spot

A-Z
DIRECTORY

It is vital to choose appropriate plants for a low-maintenance garden—some plants are more or less maintenance-free. This directory lists the best plants for a variety of situations—shade, sun, damp, and dry—and covers all the major categories of plants with which you may wish to furnish your low maintenance garden. Trees, shrubs, perennials, ground cover plants, grasses, drought-tolerant plants, bulbs, and water-lovers are all included, as is a small selection of easy edible plants. Zonal information, indicating the hardiness of the plants, is included. There is a key to the temperature ranges for the zones on page 144.

Deciduous TREES & SHRUBS

Betula utilis
H 15m (50ft) Zones 5-7
This attractive deciduous tree, commonly known as Birch, has something to offer the garden all year round. The dark green oval leaves turn a golden butter yellow before dropping in autumn and delicate yellow-brown catkins are produced in spring. In winter and early spring, the trunk and main branches display coppery-pink peeling bark that looks outstanding. Propagation is by seed sown outdoors in the fall, or cuttings taken in midsummer.

Caragana arborescens
H 6m (20ft) Zones 2-8
This small hardy tree, known as the Siberian pea tree, is ideal for screening in a larger garden as it copes well with exposed situations—it hails from Siberia and northern China. It has spiny branches and attractive light green leaves of up to 12 leaflets, with pea-like (hence the common name) pale yellow flowers in spring. It prefers well-drained soil and sun. There is a dwarf form, 'Nana' (H1.5m/5ft) which is more suitable for small garden. Propagate from greenwood cuttings in late spring.

Cotinus coggygria
H 3-5m (10-15ft) Zones 5-8
This bushy erect deciduous shrub, also known as the Smoke bush, has smallish mid-green oval leaves that turn good colours in autumn. The common name arises from the smoke-like clusters of seeds

and downy filaments that follow the insignificant flowers. It grows well in any fertile, well-drained soil in sun and can be propagated by softwood cuttings in summer or by layering in winter. 'Royal Purple' has handsome dark purple foliage, which turns brilliant red in autumn.

Crataegus
H 4.5m (15ft)
Commonly known as Hawthorn, this small tree has an open, spreading habit, with a dense thicket of twiggy stems and clusters of small, white flowers in late spring. The deeply-lobed leaves are mid-green in spring and summer, turning golden-yellow in autumn, leaving small, red berries exposed into the winter. One cultivar in particular is outstanding; *C. laevigata* 'Paul's Scarlet' (zones 5-7), which has double red flowers. Propagation is by grafting in spring or summer budding.

Hamamelis x *intermedia*
H 4m (12ft) Zones 5-9
This deciduous shrub, known as Witch hazel, has a tree-like habit. It is grown primarily for its winter flowers, which are also fragrant. The flowers have a spidery appearance and bloom on bare branches. They can be yellow, orange, or dark red, according to the variety. The leaves are broadly oval. Witch hazel grows well in most soils in sun or partial shade. *H.* x *i.* 'Pallida' has pale yellow flowers in mid to late winter.

Hypericum
H 1.2m (4ft)
Hypericum, also known as St John's wort, refers to a resilient group of deciduous or semi-evergreen shrubs with tough, light green, oval leaves. The popular cultivar, *H.* 'Hidcote' (zones 6-9) has golden-yellow, widely-opening, cup-shaped flowers produced in clusters from midsummer through until early autumn. *H.* × *inodorum* 'Elstead' (zones 7-9) also produces pinkish-red fruits in autumn, and *H.* × *moserianum* 'Tricolour' (zones 7-9) has leaves flushed cream, pink, and green. Propagation is by semi-ripe cuttings taken in summer.

Magnolia
H 5m (16ft)
Among the most spectacular flowering trees and shrubs to be found anywhere, these generally have mid-green, broadly lance-shaped leaves, often with an orange-brown, felt-like covering on the underside. The shapely, tulip-like blooms curl back on themselves to produce star-shaped white, pink or mauve flowers. *M. stellata* (zones 5-9) is a beautiful, slow-growing species with scented, clear white flowers in spring. Propagation is by layering in late spring.

Philadelphus coronarius
H 2.5m (8ft) Zones 5-8
The Mock orange produces masses of heavily scented white blooms in early and midsummer. The pale green, broadly oval leaves are a glossy mid-green and carried in

Caragana arborescens

Cotinus coggygria

opposite pairs on orange-brown stems that slowly arch over. There is also a golden leaved form of this plant, *P. c.* 'Aureus', which grows better in dappled shade. Prune by cutting back the oldest branches to ground level after flowering. Propagation is by hardwood cuttings taken in winter.

Pyrus salicifolia 'Pendula'

H 5m (l5ft) Zones 4-9

The very pretty Willow-leaved pear is a bit of a risk in a low-maintenance garden since it can be prone to a range of pests and diseases, but even low-maintenance gardeners have to live dangerously occasionally. It has wonderful silvery green fine leaves on drooping branches and creamy white flowers in spring. It makes a very attractive focal point in any garden. Grow in fertile well-drained soil in sun.

Ribes sanguineum

H 2m (7ft) Zones 6-8

The Flowering currant is one of the most reliable deciduous shrubs. It has an upright habit and its five-lobed, dark green leaves are deeply veined, turning orange-yellow in the autumn, and carried on light-brown stems. The small, open-mouthed, tubular flowers are red, pink or white, depending on the cultivar. This shrub is pruned by removing the flower-bearing shoots as flowering ends. Propagation is by hardwood cuttings taken in winter.

Salix

H5-25m (15-80ft) Zones 2-9

The willows are a large group of hardy deciduous trees and shrubs, with thin narrow, strap-like leaves carried on thin,

Hamamelis x intermedia 'Pallida'

whippy stems. Some have attractive catkin flowers, with colours ranging from creamy yellow through to a deep bluish-black. *S. alba* 'Britzensis' has orange-scarlet twigs through the winter; *S. babylonica* var. *pekinensis* has gray-green, unusually corkscrew-shaped branches; *S.* 'Tortuosa' (zones 4-9) has orange-red, contorted branches. Propagation is by hardwood cuttings, 20cm (8in) long taken in the dormant season.

Sorbus

H 1.2-15m (4-50ft) Zones 3-8

Rowans are a large family of deciduous trees and shrubs grown for their dense clusters of white flowers in spring and attractive berries that hang on the branches all winter long. *S. aucuparia* reaches up to 15m (45ft), produces bright red berries, and has leaves made up of many small mid-green leaflets that turn orange in the autumn. There is a yellow-berried form, *S. a.* 'Fructu Luteo'. Propagation is by seed sown in the autunm or grafting in the early spring.

Spiraea

H 1-3m (3-10ft) Zones 3-9

These hardy, deciduous flowering shrubs, also called Spirea, have thin and twiggy branches, starting light, orange-brown when young and aging to a dull gray. The leaves vary from narrow and spear-like through to a rounded oval, often with a puckered or corrugated margin. Leaf colour ranges from mid- to dark green. Attractive cultivars include *S. japonica* 'Goldflame', which grows to 75cm (30in) high with young golden-orange leaves, turning green as they age, with deep rose-red flowers in mid-summer. Prune out old wood as the flowers fade. Propagation is by hardwood cuttings in autumn and winter.

Pyrus salicifolia 'Pendula'

Ribes sanguineum

Crataegus laevigata 'Paul's Scarlet'

Evergreen TREES & SHRUBS

Abies koreana
H 2m (6ft) Zones 5-8
Commonly known as the Korean fir, this conifer forms a small, slow-growing tree. It has a broad, conical shape with the base of the plant being almost as wide as the height of the tree. Each needle-like leaf is dark green above, silvery white underneath. This conifer produces striking, violet-purple cones 8cm (3¹/₄in) long, even on young plants. Propagate by sowing seed into shallow pots and place outdoors in early spring.

Berberis x stenophylla

Buxus x sempervirens

Aucuba japonica
H 4m (13ft) Zones 6-10
This large, evergreen shrub, known as the Japanese laurel, will grow almost anywhere. It is equally tolerant of sun or shade. The narrowly oval leaves are a very glossy pale green when young, turning a deep green and leathery as they age, but there are a number of variegated cultivars. A. j. 'Crotonifolia' has green leaves mottled yellow, while A. j. 'Picturata' has a vivid golden splash in the centre of each green leaf. Propagation is by semi-ripe cuttings in autumn.

Berberis × stenophylla
H 2.4m (8ft) Zones 6-9
This hardy hybrid, known as Barberry, is a shrub with gracefully arching, slender branches covered with small, tough, leathery, and glossy dark-green leaves, each tipped with sharp spines. It can make an attractive specimen plant or an effective barrier as an informal flowering hedge. In late spring, vast quantities of small, orange-yellow flowers are produced, to be followed by small blue fruits. Prune by removing old shoots immediately after flowering. Propagation is by semi-ripe cuttings taken in the summer.

Buxus × sempervirens
H 5m (15ft) Zones 6-9
This, the common boxwood, makes a bushy rounded shrub or small tree (if you are around for long enough, as it is extremely slow growing). It is used most commonly for topiary, but there are various forms including more compact types ('Suffruticosa') and those with variegated leaves (such as 'Elegantissima'). Box strikes very easily from softwood cuttings in summer. It has a pungent, aromatic smell that some love, others hate. B. microphylla (small-leaved boxwood) 'Compacta' has very small leaves and grows only to 30cm (12in).

Choisya ternata
H 2m (6ft) Zones 8-10
This shrub produces dense clusters of small, white, musk-scented flowers in early summer, earning it the common name of the Mexican orange blossom. The glossy evergreen leaves are produced in whorls on green, woody stems forming a densely packed bush with a compact, dome-shaped habit. This plant needs no regular pruning but young shoots may be damaged by frost. Propagation is by semi-ripe cuttings in late summer or autumn.

Elaeagnus
H 3m (10ft) Zones 2-10
These hardy evergreen shrubs have a spreading habit and tough, leathery, broadly lance-shaped leaves, which are a rich, glossy, deep green on the upper surface and a dull silvery green on the underside. In autumn and winter, fragrant, white bell-like flowers are carried on pale-brown spiny shoots. Many cultivars are grown for their attractive variegated leaves; E. pungens 'Maculata' (zones 7-10) has a prominent golden splash in the centre of each leaf. Propagation is by semi-ripe cuttings taken late summer.

Escallonia
H 4.5m (14ft) Zones 8-10
A handsome, summer-flowering evergreen shrub, with an attractive range of flower colours, from white through pink to scarlet in late summer and autumn. Small, bell-shaped flowers are produced in clusters on short, spur-like branches above oval, glossy, dark green leaves with a pale green underside. This versatile plant can be grown as a hedge, garden shrub or wall shrub. Escallonia 'Iveyi' reaches a height of 6m (20ft) and has fragrant, pure white, tubular flowers. The plant propagates easily from softwood cuttings taken in midsummer.

Fatsia japonica
H 3m (10ft) Zones 7-10
This handsome evergreen, known as Japanese aralia or Japanese fatsia, has large, leathery, seven-lobed leaves and is an

Choisya ternata

excellent choice for a shady town garden, where it will cope well with pollution and even salty winds by the seaside. It has creamy white umbels (small balls) of flowers in autumn, followed by small black fruit. Grow it in dappled shade or full sun. Propagate from greenwood cuttings in early summer.

Ilex
H 5m (15ft) Zones 6-9
All the hollies produce white, star-shaped flowers in late spring or early summer, but they often go unnoticed, with red, orange, yellow or even white berries being produced on the female plants throughout the winter. The leaves may vary in colour but have the sharp spines around the margin. This is a plant which can be grown as a hedge or as a small tree. Propagation is by semi-ripe cuttings taken in August.

Mahonia aquifolium
H 1m (3ft) Zones 5-9
The Oregon grape is a tough shrub of spreading, suckering habit, which is ideal for ground cover. In spring, the strongly scented flowers are rich yellow and carried in dense clusters on the shoot tips. The glossy, dark green, leathery leaves are made up of up to nine leaflets, often turning bright crimson around the margins in autumn and winter. A cultivar well worth growing is M. a. 'Apollo', which has deep green leaves and bright yellow flowers. Propagate by taking suckers in late autumn.

Picea pungens
H 15m (45ft) Zones 3-8
The Colorado spruce has a broadly columnar habit and orange-brown shoots

Escallonia 'Iveyi'

developing purplish-gray bark as they age. The bluish, gray-green, slightly curved, needle-like leaves have a thin, bluish, waxy covering. The young cones are green, later turning brown with age. The popular, slow-growing P. p. 'Koster' is an attractive cultivar with silvery blue leaves and stiff arching branches. Propagation is by grafting indoors in the spring.

Pyracantha
H 5m (15ft) Zones 6-9
The Firethorn forms a naturally spreading shrub that makes an excellent hedge, free-standing shrub or wall shrub. The small, evergreen leaves are a bright, glossy green with a finely toothed margin, carried on stout, thorny, upright shoots. In early

Fatsia japonica

summer, huge clusters of small, white, star-shaped flowers are produced, followed in autumn and winter by yellow, orange or bright red berries, depending on the cultivar. Propagation is by semi-ripe cuttings taken in autumn.

Rhododendron yakushimanum
H 2m (6ft) Zones 5-9
This very hardy shrub originates from Japan and makes a tightly dome-shaped bush with dark green, glossy leaves in mid-spring. It has deep pink, funnel shaped flowers that fade to white. R. 'Ken Janeck' is smaller (1.2m/4ft) with white flowers. It needs moist, well-drained, acidic soil. Propagate by semi-ripe cuttings in later summer.

Mahonia aquifolium 'Apollo'

Picea pungens 'Koster'

PLANTS FOR EASY HEDGES
Berberis x stenophylla
Buxus
Carpinus
Chamaecyparis
Elaeagnus
Escallonia
Fagus
Griselinia
Ilex
Ligustrum
Lonicera
Prunus (Laurel)
Pyracantha
Taxus
Thuja
Viburnum tinus

CLIMBERS & WALL SHRUBS

Campsis × tagliabuana
H 10m (30ft) Zones 5-9
The Trumpet vine is ideal for vertical gardening up sunny walls, fences, pergolas, gazebos or other upright structures. The leaves, carried on gray-green stems, are light to mid-green in colour and made up of a number of smaller leaflets that turn golden-yellow in the autumn. From late summer until early autumn, orange-red trumpet-like flowers are carried in clusters on the shoot tips. Propagate by taking root cuttings in early spring.

Clematis 'Jackmanii Superba'
H 3m (10ft) Zones 4-9
A hybrid clematis with large matte green leaves modified at the tips to form self-clinging tendrils. From midsummer onwards, large violet-purple flowers with yellowish-brown centres are produced on the new shoots. Pruning consists of cutting the plants down to 30cm (12in) each spring, and the plant can be increased by cuttings in summer. Other clematis, such as the *C. viticella* hybrids can be grown in the same way and offer some resistance to clematis wilt disease.

Clematis montana var. rubens
H 12m (40ft) Zones 3-9
This vigorous, reliable plant is one of the easiest climbers to grow, because it will survive almost anywhere, and produce an excellent display. The lovely four-petaled flowers are pale pink in colour and emerge from late spring into early summer. The young shoots and tendrils are often a dull red colour, aging to a dark purple-tinted green. No regular pruning is required. The plant is easy to grow from cuttings and resistant to most pests and diseases. *C.m.* 'Odorata' has the bonus of scented flowers.

Cytisus battandieri
H 4m (13ft) Zones 7-10
The spectacular Pineapple broom is a wall shrub with outstanding flowers arranged in pineapple-scented, golden-yellow spikes from early to midsummer. The semi-evergreen foliage is mid-green (with a silvery sheen created by a soft, white felt-like covering over its leaves and young shoots). It tolerates a range of conditions, but grows best when given some protection from cold winds. Propagation is by semi-ripe cuttings taken in late summer.

Garrya elliptica
H 2.4m (8ft) Zones 7-10
This tough evergreen, known as the Silk tassel bush, is an ideal shrub for walls and fences. Its leaves are thick, leathery, and oval-shaped with a slightly crinkled margin. They are dark green in colour with a glossy upper surface, and a slightly blue sheen on the underside, carried on erect gray-green branches. Long strands of small bell-like flowers form attractive drooping catkins in the spring. *G. e.* 'James Roof' has the longest, most colourful catkins. Propagate by taking hardwood cuttings in autumn.

Hedera helix
H 10m (33ft) Zones 3-8
The ivy is a vigorous, evergreen, self-clinging climber, ideal for covering walls. The leaves vary in shape and size according to age, and many cultivars are grown for their attractive variegated leaf colours. Forms include the golden-leaved *H. h.* 'Buttercup', and the dark-purple leaved *H. h.* 'Atropurpurea'. This plant needs little attention, as it supports itself by clinging tendrils and requires next to no pruning. Propagation is by semi-ripe cuttings taken in late summer.

Humulus lupulus
H 8m (26ft) Zones 4-8
This attractive and self-supporting, herbaceous perennial climber, known as hops, has thin, bristly, twining stems. The equally bristly leaves are toothed around the margins and have deep lobes. In summer, insignificant green flowers are produced, followed in autumn by attractive clusters of fruit (hops). The most popular form is *H. l.* 'Aureus', a clone with soft golden-yellow leaves and stems. The variety *H. l.* 'Variegata' is a less vigorous form, with creamy white and green variegated leaves. Propagation is by semi-ripe cuttings taken in June and July.

Jasminum nudiflorum
H 3m (10ft) Zones 6-9
The popular Winter jasmine is an outstanding wall shrub. Its whippy stems are square in shape and green in colour, which gives the plant an evergreen appearance. Its

Campsis x tagliabuana

Clematis montana 'Odorata'

Garrya elliptica

small, fragrant, tubular yellow flowers open from November until April to form a five-petalled star. The variegated form, *J. n.* 'Aureum', has golden-yellow splashes on the leaves. This plant can be grown from semi-ripe cuttings taken in September.

Lonicera peryclimenum
H 3m (10ft) Zones 5-9

This attractive, twining climber, also known as the common honeysuckle, has fragrant, tubular flowers, carried individually or in clusters, on new shoots from mid- to late summer. Flower colours range from white through pale yellow to gold, pink, and scarlet. Leaves vary in shape from broadly oval to almost circular and in colour from pale to mid-green. Prune by cutting back lateral shoots in spring, and removing old wood after flowering. Propagation is by hardwood cuttings taken in winter.

Parthenocissus tricuspidata
H 9m (30ft) Zones 4-8

Also known as Boston ivy, this is a vigorous and attractive self-clinging climber which is ideal for covering walls. The leaves vary in shape and size according to age. Leaf colour starts as mid- to dark green in summer, changing to a dramatic blazing scarlet in autumn. The young purple shoots remain stuck to the wall by small sucker pads after the leaves have fallen. Small greenish-yellow flowers are produced in summer. Propagate by taking semi-ripe cuttings in summer.

Rosa 'Albertine'
H 5m (15ft) Zones 5-9

One of the most reliable rambler roses ever produced, this is a vigorous grower on a wall, trellis or fence, where it will need tying into place. The young growths produce coppery orange leaves that later turn a glossy mid-green on dull red shoots. The flowers are lobster pink, open, with a golden centre, fading with age. Prune by cutting out the old flower-bearing shoots. Propagation is by hardwood cuttings taken in late autumn.

Rosa xanthina 'Canary Bird'
H 3m (10ft) Zones 5-9

Like many species roses, *R. xanthina* 'Canary Bird' is fairly resistant to the usual ailments that plague roses. It has red-flushed stems, small ferny leaves, and small single yellow flowers that have a musky scent. It does best in fertile soil in full sun. Other good roses for the low-maintenance garden, which also make good informal hedges, are the rugosa roses. *R. rugosa* 'Rosea' has pretty rose-pink flowers, while *R.r.* 'Alba' has white ones. The flowers are scented and are followed by large red hips.

Schizophragma integrifolium
H 12m (40ft) Zones 6-9

This tough climber, which hails from Asia, has showy white flowers, similar to those of the lacecap hydrangea, in summer. The leaves are pointed ovals, dark green in colour. It attaches itself to its support by means of aerial roots. It is pest- and disease-free. Grow it in moist well-rained soil in partial shade or full sun. Propagate from semi-ripe cuttings in late summer.

Solanum crispum 'Glasnevin'
H 4m (13ft) Zones 8-10

One of the most attractive wall shrubs, the Chilean potato vine makes a splendid display, with its large, mop-head clusters of small, star-shaped, deep blue flowers produced through summer and autumn. The leaves have a glossy, dark green upper surface with a paler underside, and turn bright yellow in the autumn. The erect stems are a bright, glossy green, even through the winter. Prune by cutting back untidy growths in spring or summer. This plant can be increased by taking semi-ripe cuttings in early summer.

EASY-CARE TIP

When selecting a climbing plant, try to choose one that is self-supporting (twining stems, tendrils, etc). These may need some extra training in the early stages, but will require very little artificial support, such as hooks or wires, once they become established.

Humulus lupulus 'Aureus'

Rosa xanthina 'Canary Bird'

Schizophragma integrifolium

GROUND COVER PLANTS FOR SUN

Alchemilla mollis
H 45cm (18in) Zones 4-7
This low-growing, herbaceous perennial, also known as Lady's mantle, has a dense, clump-forming habit and attractive foliage. It hates wet soil conditions. The leaves are a felty bluish-green, shallowly notched with a serrated margin. Tall sprays of star-shaped, lime green flowers appear in midsummer carried on thin, green felt-covered stems. Propagate by division in autumn or seed sown in spring, although this plant will frequently self-seed in a garden.

Anthemis punctata ssp. cupaniana
H 30cm (12in) Zones 6-9
This evergreen plant is invaluable for a dry, sunny garden. It forms a loose cushion of finely cut, silvery gray, aromatic foliage that turns green in winter. The white, daisy-like flowers have a golden centre, or 'eye', and are carried singly above the leaves on short erect stems in July and August. No regular pruning is required but dead flower heads are usually removed in autumn. Propagate by semi-ripe basal cuttings taken in summer.

Artemisia
H up to 1.2m (4ft) Zones 3-9
Many of these plants, also known as Wormwood, are herbaceous perennials and others are shrubs. At times, it can be very difficult to tell which is which. They are usually grown for their aromatic, silver-gray foliage. One very popular plant is A. 'Powis Castle' (zones 6-9), a woody-based perennial reaching about 60cm (2ft) in height. The thin, silver-clad twigs are covered with a mound of feathery, silver-gray leaves and small yellow-tinged silvery flower heads in summer. This plant may be damaged by severe cold. Propagate by semi-ripe basal cuttings taken in summer.

Bergenia cordifolia
H 30cm (12in) Zones 3-8
This hardy evergreen perennial, commonly known as Elephant's ears, has bold, tough, rounded, mid-green leathery leaves with a heart-shaped base. They look particularly attractive in warm winters when orange and yellow tints are found on the leaf edges. In spring, bell-shaped, white, red, or lilac-pink flowers are carried on erect red-tinted stems. B.c. 'Purpurea' has magenta flowers and redder leaves. The leaves of Bergenia crassifolia are smaller than B. cordifolia. They are tinged with red in winter. Propagate by division in early autumn.

Erigeron
H 60cm (2ft) Zones 3-8
These clump-forming herbaceous perennials, also known as Fleabane, are excellent for covering soil. They have mid-green, oblong or spoon-shaped leaves growing out in a tangled rosette from the base of the plant. In summer, yellow-centreed, daisy-like flowers come in shades of pink, blue or white carried on slender green stems. There are a number of handsome cultivars, such as E. 'Darkest of All', with its violet-blue flowers, or 'Gaiety', which is a bright pink. Propagate by division after flowering or in early spring.

Euphorbia myrsinites
H 10cm (4in) Zones 5-8
This evergreen perennial, also called Myrtle spurge, has snake-like semi-prostrate stems covered in succulent silver green leaves which are covered, at their tips in spring, with bright greenish yellow flowers. It does best in light soil in full sun. Root sections of stem in spring. Can be prone to gray mould and mealybugs. The sap can sometimes cause skin irritation.

Geranium 'Johnson's Blue'
H 45cm (18in) Zones 4-8
This low-growing perennial has a dome-shaped, spreading habit. The mid-green, deeply incised leaves have a scalloped margin, and are held above the ground on thin green leaf stalks. The saucer-shaped flowers have five petals, and are lavender-blue with clearly marked veins within each petal. This cultivar is very free-flowering and will tolerate a wide range of growing

Alchemillia mollis

Artemisia 'Powis Castle'

Bergenia crassifolia

conditions. The leaves often turn orange before dying back in the autumn. Propagate by division in early spring.

Hebe

H up to 1m (3ft) Zones 8-11
There are a number of dome-shaped, low-growing evergreen hebes that make excellent ground cover shrubs, as they tend to shade their own roots, which helps them to tolerate dry conditions. *Hebe albicans* forms a dense mound of thick, gray-green leaves up to 60cm (2ft) high, capped with white flowers in midsummer. *H. pinguifolia* 'Pagei' has a low, spreading habit, forming a thick carpet of blue-green leaves 30cm (1ft) high, splashed with white flowers in late-spring and early summer. Propagate by detaching rooted shoot sections in autumn or taking semi-ripe cuttings in late-summer.

Heuchera micrantha

H up to 90cm (3ft) Zones 4-8
This mound-forming herbaceous perennial, also called Coral flower, has heart-shaped, hairy leaves with lobed margins, coloured mid-green mottled with gray. It bears long spikes of pinkish-white flowers in early summer. An interesting cultivar is *H. m.* 'Purple Palace', which has metallic, bronze-red foliage and creamy green flowers reaching up to 45cm (18in), followed by rose-pink seed heads by late-summer. Propagate by division in early autumn.

Juniperus

H 1-5m (3-15ft) Zones 2-10
Junipers are versatile, hardy conifers that come in a vast array of cultivars selected for growth forms and habits or different foliage colours. The low-growing 'prostrate' cultivars grow rapidly, and make good ground cover for low-maintenance gardens. Once established, they can be left very much to their own devices. *J. x pftizeriana* 'Wilhelm Pfitzer' is a spreading, flat-topped shrub with gray-green leaves. *J. x p.* 'Pfitzeriana Aurea' has golden foliage. Propagate by semi-ripe cuttings taken in autumn.

Persicaria vaccinifolia

H 20cm (8in) Zones
This low-growing evergreen perennial creeps over the ground, forming a dense mat of small, glossy green, spear-shaped leaves, tinted with a red margin in cold weather. The stems also have red markings and will root freely wherever they come into contact with the soil. In late summer and early autumn, slender, upright spikes of deep-pink flowers are carried above the carpet of leaves. This plant prefers full sunlight. Propagate by division in spring or autumn.

Saxifraga x urbium

H 30cm (12in) Zones 6-7
This evergreen saxifrage, known as London pride, is one of more than 400 species in this genus. It makes good ground cover even in poor soil, and does best in moist soil in partial shade. A vigorous grower, it forms rosettes of evergreen leaves from which tall stems of pinkish white star-shaped flowers are borne in summer. To propagate, detach individual rosettes and root in autumn.

Veronica prostrata

H to 15cm (6in) Zones 5-8
This very low-growing evergreen plant, known as Speedwell, forms a dense, flat mat over the soil surface. The flowers are small and bright blue, arranged in spikes on short stems in spring and summer. Propagate by detaching rooted shoot sections in spring or taking cuttings in summer.

Geranium 'Johnson's Blue'

Juniperus x *pftizeriana* 'Pfitzeriana Aurea'

Euphorbia myrsinites

Saxifraga x *urbium*

GROUND COVER PLANTS FOR SHADE

Ajuga reptans
H 15cm (6in) Zones 3-9
This low-growing evergreen perennial is commonly known as Carpet bugle or common bugle. It has dark green, spoon-shaped leaves, colonizes areas very quickly, and copes well with poor soil. Its vigorous horizontal stems form a dense mat with spikes of dark blue flowers in late spring and early summer. Several cultivars have variegated leaves. *A. r.* 'Burgundy Glow' has attractive wine-coloured leaves. Propagate this plant by dividing rooted stems in early spring.

Brunnera macrophylla
H 45cm (18in) Zones 4-8
A low-growing plant, Siberian bugloss has roughly textured, heart-shaped, slightly hairy, matte green leaves. In late spring and early summer, delicate sprays of small, star-shaped bright blue flowers with an orange-yellow eye in the centre are produced. *B. m.* 'Dawson's White' has attractive white variegated leaves. Propagation is either by division in the spring or seed sown in the autumn.

Campanula carpatica
H 30cm (1ft) Zones 5-9
The Bellflower is a low-growing, clump-forming herbaceous perennial with smooth, broadly oval to heart-shaped, mid-green leaves, held on mid-green stems. It does best in well-drained soil in partial shade. The pretty single flowers are openly bell-shaped, coloured white, blue or violet-purple and held upright on the stems from midsummer until early autumn. There are several popular named cultivars of the species plant, with *C. c.* 'Bressingham White' having larger flowers. Propagation is by division in autumn after the plants have flowered, although this plant will frequently self-seed in a garden.

Epimedium grandiflorum
H 30cm (1ft) Zones 5-8
These low-growing, hardy, deciduous plants, also called Barrenwort, are superb as ground cover in partial shade. The leaves are almost heart-shaped, and are bright green, tinted pinkish red when young, darkening with age. In autumn, these leaves display vivid tints of yellow, orange, red, and bronze, carried on thin woody leaf stalks. The clusters of small, cup-shaped flowers are produced in spring and summer, in colours ranging from white to mauve, depending on the cultivar. A good cultivar is *E.g.* 'White Queen' with pure white flowers. Propagate by division in early spring.

Hedera helix
H 15cm (6in) Zones 3-8
This low-growing, self-clinging or trailing evergreen, commonly known as Ivy, is the most useful plant of all for really deep shade. It grows well in very poor, dry soil. There is a huge range of species and varieties to choose from, from those with tiny starry tri-lobed leaves to ones with much larger variegated leaves. Ivies vary greatly in vigour so you need to choose one appropriate for the position. *H.hibernica* (zones 5-9) will make fast-growing ground cover. Propagate this plant by division in spring or autumn.

Lamium maculatum
H 20cm (8in) Zones 3-9
A low-growing relative of the deadnettle, the Spotted deadnettle creeps both over the ground and under it, spreading rapidly once it has become established. This is a useful fast growing plant which tolerates shade. The mid-green leaves are coarsely textured, broadly heart-shaped with a deeply toothed margin—although a number of cultivars are grown for their silver, gold, or white variegated leaves. Clusters of hooded flowers, varying in colour from reddish-purple, to pink or white, depending on the cultivar, are borne in mid-spring. Propagation is by division in the autumn or early spring.

Pachyphragma macrophyllum
H 40cm (16in) Zones 5-9
This semi-evergreen perennial has creeping underground stems, which form a dense clump. The glossy green leaves are oval-shaped with a deeply notched margin, carried on green stems. From early spring until midsummer, dense clusters of pure

Ajuga reptans

Campanula carpatica 'Jewel'

Epimedium grandiflorum 'Rose Queen'

white, cross-shaped flowers are produced, followed by flat seed pods in the autumn. The plant likes fertile to moist soil and partial shade. Propagation is by division or seed sown in the autumn, although this plant will frequently self-seed in a garden.

Petasites japonicus
H 45cm (18in) Zones 5-9
This large-leaved perennial does best in damp shade. It grows naturally alongside streams. The large heart- to kidney-shaped leaves are up to 30in (76cm) across. Large yellowish white flowerheads, with a characteristic cluster of flowers surrounded by pointed bracts, are borne in spring. Propagate this plant by division in spring or autumn.

Rubus tricolor
H 20cm (8in) Zones 3-8
This evergreen plant is invaluable for a dry garden. It forms a loose cushion of finely cut, silvery grey, aromatic foliage, which turns green in the winter. The white daisy-like flowers have a golden centre, or 'eye', and are carried singly above the leaves on short erect stems in July and August. No regular pruning is required but dead flower heads are usually removed in autumn. Propagation is by semi-ripe basal cuttings taken in the summer.

Tellima grandiflora
H 45cm (18in) Zones 4-8
This hardy herbaceous plant, also called Fringe cups, flowers from late spring until midsummer. Slender, erect stems carry small, bell-like flowers, initially of a yellow-green, later tinged pink. Originating from the base of the plant, the light green, hairy leaves are heart-shaped or triangular with a deeply notched margin. Propagate this plant by division in spring or seed sown in autumn.

Tiarella cordifolia
H 45cm (18in) Zones 3-8
This pretty plant, known commonly as the foam flower, has attractive, bright, heart-shaped green leaves that are tinted bronze in autumn. It spreads by stolons and likes cool, moist, rich soil and copes well even with deep shade. Creamy white flowers are borne in summer on long spikes and the leaves turn an attractive bronze red in autumn. *T. wherryi* (zones 6-10) is similar, but smaller. Propagate this plant by division in spring.

Vinca major
H 40cm (16in) Zones 7-11
Commonly known as the greater periwinkle, this tough little plant has a low,

Lamium maculatum

Petasites japonicus

Tiarella wherryi

spreading habit and produces star-shaped, violet-blue flowers continuously from mid-spring until autumn. It does well in any but very dry soil and copes well with partial shade, although it flowers most profusely in full sun. Slender, tough green stems creep across the soil bearing spear-shaped, dark green leaves, although there are cultivars with white or golden variegated margins to the leaves, and others with yellow centres to their green leaves. There are also cultivars with purple or white flowers. Propagation is by division in spring and autumn or semi-ripe cuttings in summer.

Waldsteinia ternata
H 15cm (6in) Zones 3-8
This is a vigorous, spreading, evergreen perennial with a dense, tufted habit. The deep green, coarsely textured leaves are composed of three leaflets and shallowly lobed. In late spring and early summer, small clusters of bright yellow, saucer-shaped, buttercup-like flowers are produced on slender green stems. This plant will flourish in a dry, shaded position, and is ideal for a bank, but it may become invasive. Propagate by seed sown in autumn and spring or division in spring.

GRASSES AND SEDGES

Arundo donax
H 5m (16ft) Zones 6-10
Originating from southern Europe, the Giant reed has long, gray-green leaves that splay out from long stems, making it ideal for the back of a border. Spikes of greenish-purple flowers are produced in mid- to late autumn. Prune by cutting to ground level in the spring. There is also an attractive slower-growing form, *A. d.* 'Versicolor', with white margins to the leaves. Propagation is by division in spring.

Briza media
H 60cm (2ft) Zones 4-10
This is an attractive, evergreen perennial grass, known as Common quaking grass, grown for its narrow, blue-green leaves growing up to 40cm (16in) long and forming a dense mound-like clump. Throughout summer, spikes of purplish, heart-shaped flowers are produced above the leaves on long slender stems. In autumn, the flowers turn a golden straw colour and are ideal in indoor arrangements. This plant will grow equally well in full sun or partial shade. Propagation is by division in spring.

Calamagrostis × acutiflora
H 1.5m (5ft) Zones 5-9
The attractive, clump-forming Feather reed grass has a vigorous, upright habit. The slightly glossy, mid-green leaves reach up to 1m (3ft) tall. In mid- to late summer, tall slender stems carry delicate, pinkish-brown flower heads which slowly die, but remain on the plant well into the winter, providing interest over a longer period. The cultivar *C. × a.* 'Overdam' has yellow stripes in the leaves. Propagate by division in spring.

Carex elata 'Aurea'
H up to 40cm (16in) Zones 5-9
Although this plant is a deciduous perennial sedge, rather than a true grass, it is often grown among grasses and treated as a grass. Commonly known as Bowles' golden sedge, it forms a dense clump of rich yellow- and green-striped leaves that gently arch from the centre of the plant. In late spring or early summer, brown male flowers are carried on long, slender stems, with green female flowers just below them. This plant prefers a moist fertile soil and is propagated by division in spring.

Carex pendula
H 1m (3ft) Zones 5-9
Also called Weeping sedge, this is an evergreen, tuft-forming, graceful perennial sedge with narrow green leaves and solid triangular stems that freely produce pendent greenish brown flower spikes in summer. This plant prefers partial shade. Propagate by division in spring.

Cortaderia selloana
H 2.4m (8ft) Zones 7-10
This very popular ornamental grass, also known as Pampas grass or Silver comet, is a clump-forming, evergreen perennial, with long, coarse, finely toothed, olive-green leaves up to 1.2m (4ft) long. Tall stems carry long, shaggy plumed flowers from midsummer onwards. There are a number of different forms, including *C. s.* 'Rendatleri' (pink flowers), *C. s.* 'Sunningdale Silver' (silvery-white flowers) and *C. s.* 'Aureolineata' (yellow margins to the leaves). This plant can be pruned by cutting back the leaves with shears in spring and is propagated in spring by division.

Festuca glauca
H 30cm (1ft) Zones 4-8
Although the 'Blue fescue' is a close relative of many lawn grasses, its tufted habit makes it totally unsuitable for lawns. It eventually forms a hummock of blue-gray leaves up to twice as wide as its height. The flowers are blue-green flushed with violet, carried from late spring on thin stems. Notable cultivars include *F. g.* 'Harz', which has blue-green leaves tipped purple. Propagation is by division in spring.

Hakonechloa macra
H 40cm (16in) Zones 5-9
This smooth-leaved, deciduous, perennial grass forms a loose mound of arching, overlapping leaves, often giving it a very unkempt and shaggy appearance. In late summer it produces spikes of pale green flowers, which are quite insignificant and often hidden by the foliage. The variegated form *H. m.* 'Aureola', is very attractive with bright yellow leaves with a rich green stripe that age to reddish-brown. Reddish brown

Calamagrostis x acutiflora

Cortaderia selloana 'Sunningdale Silver'

Miscanthus sinensis

flower spikes may appear in early autumn and last into winter. For the best leaf colour, variegated plants should be grown in partial shade. Propagation is by division in spring.

Helictotrichon sempervirens

H 1.2m (4ft) Zones 4-9

The fine, evergreen Blue oat grass has steely, gray-blue leaves that may be rolled or broad and flat and up to 25cm (10in) long. This plant is ideal for a sunny position with a fertile, well-drained soil. In early to midsummer, stiff erect stems carry graceful, nodding spikes of straw-coloured, purple-flecked flowers. Prune by removing old, dead leaves and flower spikes in the spring. Propagation is by seed sown under protection in the spring or by division in the spring.

Imperata cylindrica 'Rubra'

H 45cm (18in) Zones 4-9

This deciduous, perennial grass, also known as Japanese blood grass, has broad, flat leaves that start out as a dull, mid-green, but gradually change to a vivid red from the tip down to the base of each leaf blade, forming a loose, glowing clump. The silvery, plume-like flowers are produced on the tips of slender stems in late summer. It prefers partial shade and a soil that does not dry out. Propagation is by division in the spring or early summer.

Lagurus ovatus

H 45cm (18in) Zones

Also called Hare's tail, this tuft-forming annual bears dense, egg-shaped soft panicles of white flower spikes with golden stamens in summer that last well into autumn. The leaves are long, narrow and flat. This grass likes a sunny position and it self-seeds readily.

Milium effusum 'Aureum'

H 60cm (2ft) Zones 5-9

This is a short-lived, semi-evergreen grass, also known as Golden wood millet, that forms a loose mound and slowly spreads to cover small areas of the garden. Every part of the plant is bright yellow, from the soft, smooth leaves to the flowers and seed heads, but the colour pales if the plant is grown in shade. Flowering starts in mid-spring and continues until late summer. Propagation is not usually necessary, as this plant self-seeds quite happily in shade to keep replacing the parent plant.

Miscanthus sinensis

H 1.8m (6ft) Zones 4-9

This vigorous, clump-forming ornamental grass, commonly known as Eulalia grass, is grown for its attractive, bold, glossy leaves, but it has the advantage of being able to grow almost anywhere, and is more than capable of taking care of itself. The flower heads appear between midsummer and mid-autumn, and there are now at least 40 different forms of this plant. Notable cultivars include *M. s.* 'Gracillimus', which has narrow white leaf margins, often turning bronze, sometimes bearing panicles of white spikelets in early autumn, and *M. s.* 'Zebrinus' (with pale yellow horizontal bands across the leaves). Propagate by division in the spring, as the new growth starts.

Stipa gigantea

H 2m (6½ft) Zones

A glorious plant for growing as a specimen. This evergreen grass, also known as Giant feather grass, forms a dense, tufted mound of long, narrow, rolled mid-green leaves often 75cm (30in) long. In summer, long slender stems carry large oat-like flowers (hence the name), which turn golden as they age, and last on the plant throughout the winter. Prune by cutting down the flower stems in spring. Propagation is by seed sown under protection in the spring or by division in the late-spring or early summer.

Milium effusum 'Aureum'

Hakonechloa macra 'Aureola'

Stipa gigantea

PERENNIALS THAT DON'T NEED STAKING

Acanthus spinosus

H 1.5m (5ft) Zones 5-9

Bear's breeches has large leaves, which are a glossy dark-green, strap-like, and armed with sharp spines on the points of the toothed margin. Appearing from late-spring until midsummer, the tall elegant spikes of white and purple flowers are carried on sturdy green stems, sandwiched between layers of green spiny bracts. This plant is pruned by removing the dead flowers and stalks when flowering has finished. Propagate by taking root cuttings in early spring, or by division in winter.

Dicentra spectabilis

H 75cm (30in) Zones 3-9

This colourful herbaceous perennial, known as Bleeding heart, has fleshy, pinkish-red stems and pale-green, deeply-lobed leaves. From late-spring until early summer, slender arching stems carry trusses of deep pink, heart-shaped flowers with white inner petals, which dangle and sway in the breeze high above the leaves. The white-flowered form, D. s. alba, blooms until midsummer and is more sturdy than the pink-flowered form. Propagation is by root cuttings in the winter, or division in the early spring.

Dierama pulcherrimum

H 1.5m (5ft) Zones

A clump-forming evergreen perennial with long, sword-like, mid-green leaves, commonly known as Angel's fishing rod. In midsummer, long, slender, arching stems carry sprays of dangling, bell-shaped, deep pink flowers, followed by round, light brown, capsule-like seed pods. This plant prefers a moist free-draining soil, but is slow to establish. The cultivar D. p. 'Blackbird' produces flowers that are deep purple in colour. Propagation is by division in the spring or seed sown after frosts in spring.

Geum chiloense 'Lady Stratheden'

H 60cm (2ft) Zones 5-9

A clump-forming, tough herbaceous perennial, Avens has deeply veined, coarse, hairy leaves, which are lobed and toothed around the margins. Slender green stems carry saucer-like crimson flowers throughout the summer. There are some notable hybrids, including G. 'Lady Stratheden' with semi-double, butter-yellow flowers, and G. 'Mrs Bradshaw' with semi-

double scarlet flowers. Propagation for the hybrids is by division in autumn and spring, or for G. chiloense, seed sown after the risk of frost has passed in spring .

Helenium autumnale

H 1.5m (5ft) Zones 4-8

This clump-forming, tall perennial, known commonly as Sneezeweed, has bright yellow daisy flowers with brown centres (disc florets) from midsumer to late autumn. Other good gold cultivars include H. 'Goldrausch' and H. 'Sonnenwunder'. Burnt orange cultivars include H. 'Moerheim Beauty' (slightly smaller at lm/3ft) and H. 'Septemberfuchs'. Grow in moist soil in full sun. Propagate by division in autumn or spring. These plants are generally trouble-free, although prone to leaf spot.

Helleborus orientalis

H 45cm(18in) Zones 4-9

This hardy evergreen perennial forms a compact mound of tough leathery leaves, which are mid- to dark green but paler beneath, carried on thick, pale green stems. In the winter, each flower head is made up of several cup-shaped, white or creamy green blooms, produced at the shoot tip. These stems are cut back after flowering has finished, to prune the plant. Propagation is by seed sown in the summer and placed in a cold frame.

Iris unguicularis

H 30cm (12in) Zones

Also known as the Algerian iris, or Winter iris, this is a vigorous, clump-forming, evergreen herbaceous perennial with tough, narrow, strap-like leaves. The large, fragrant flowers vary in colour from white through pale lavender to deep violet blue with yellow marking and dark veins, and they are held above the leaves on dark green stems from late winter to early spring. The buds are prone to attack by slugs. The cultivar I. u. 'Alba' has creamy white flowers with yellow markings. The plant prefers a sheltered site against a south- or west-facing wall. Propagation is by division in the spring soon after the flowers have died down.

Meconopsis cambrica

H 45cm (18in) Zones 6-8

A colourful, herbaceous perennial, the Welsh poppy has bluish-green hairy leaves which are deeply and irregularly lobed, often making the plant look quite untidy. The orange-yellow flowers are cup-shaped, carried on the tips of slender, green, hairy stems from mid-spring right through until the autumn. There are double-flowered yellow and orange forms, and M. 'Francis Perry' has large scarlet flowers. Propagation is by division in the autumn soon after flowering has finished.

Acanthus spinosus

Geum 'Lady Stratheden'

Ophiopogon planiscapus 'Nigrescens'

H 25cm (10in) Zones 6-10

This low-growing evergreen perennial plant has arching clusters of narrow strap-like leaves, which are a deep purplish-black, often giving the plant an untidy appearance as it forms a dense thicket. In summer the short sprays of tiny whitish-mauve, bell-like flowers are scattered among the leaves, and are followed by shiny blue-black berries by the autumn. The young leaves may be prone to slug damage in the spring. Propagation is by division in the spring.

Papaver

H 15-90cm Zones 2-9

Poppies come in many forms, single, semi-double, and double flowered—the annuals are weeds in fields and roadsides. The alpine poppies are smaller, while variants of the field poppy (*P. rhoeas*) are larger.
P. r. 'Mother of Pearl' is one of the taller poppies with soft pink or grayish blue flowers. *P. orientale* 'Cedric Morris' has larger pale pink flowers with a prominent dark eye. Poppies need full sun and fertile soil. Sow seed in spring. Can be prone to aphids and downy mildew.

Phlomis tuberosa

H lm (3ft) Zones 6-9

This is one of a number of perennials in this genus, which also includes evergreen shrubs such as *P. fruticosa* (Jerusalem sage). They make excellent mound-forming clumps with sage-like, gray-green, long narrow leaves, and nettle-like flowers. *P. cashmeriana* has purplish-pink flowers, as does *P. tuberosa*. *P. fruticosa* has bright yellow flowers and is evergreen. Grow in well-drained soil in full sun. Divide perennials in spring.

Physalis alkekengi var. franchetii

H 60-75cm (24-30in) Zones 5-8

Chinese lantern is a fast-growing herbaceous perennial with a spreading habit. The mid-green leaves are triangular in shape, carried on erect green stems, with small, white, bell-shaped flowers produced in the leaf joints during the summer. This plant is grown mainly for its decorative orange-red, papery, lantern-like structures that encase orange, yellow or purple berries, and will often hang on the plant all winter. Propagate by sowing seed or dividing in spring.

Scabiosa

H 60cm (2ft) Zones 3-9

A clump-forming herbaceous perennial plant with leaves that are strap-like, with the upper part divided into narrow segments forming a low, clustered rosette. Daisy-like flowers, ranging from white to blue to

Helenium 'Moerheim Beauty'

Meconopsis cambrica

Papaver rhoeas 'Mother of Pearl'

mauves and pinks, are borne on long slender stems. Popular forms are the lavender-blue flowered *S.* 'Butterfly Blue', and *S.* 'Pink Mist' with its deep pink flower heads, while the much older *S. caucasica* 'Miss Willmott' is the most popular white cultivar. Propagate by taking softwood cuttings in spring and summer, or division in spring.

Schizostylis coccinea

H 40cm (16in) Zones 7-9

This evergreen perennial, also known as Crimson flag, has long, narrow, strap-like leaves and spikes of open cup-shaped scarlet flowers held above the leaves on slender green stems in autumn. *S. c.* 'Major' has larger scarlet flowers in late summer, *S. c.* 'Alba' produces white flowers, while *S. c.* 'Jennifer' has mid-pink flowers, 'Sunrise' is salmon-pink, and 'Vicountess Byng' produces pale-pink flowers in late autumn. These plants should be planted in groups to create the best effect. Propagate by division in spring.

Phlomis tuberosa

SMALL PERENNIALS FOR DROUGHT

Alyssum spinosum
H 30cm (12in) Zones 5-8
This plant naturally forms a low, dense mound spreading to about 60cm (24in) in diameter. The small leaves are silvery-gray in colour and form a dense cover over the thin, shrubby, spine-tipped stems. In early summer, clusters of pure-white flowers are carried above the leaves in slender arching spikes. In addition to the white-flowered form there is also a rose-pink flowered variety; *A. s.* var *roseum*. Propagation is by semi-ripe cuttings taken in early spring.

Armeria maritima
H 15cm (6in) Zones 4-8
This mound-forming evergreen perennial has narrow, strap-like, dark green leaves. The compact flower heads can vary greatly in colour, ranging from white, through shades of pink to a reddish-purple. This plant is very adaptable, being able to cope with drought, extremely cold temperatures as well as salt-laden air. Propagation is by seed or division in early spring.

Calamintha nepeta
H 30cm (12in) Zones 5-9
This is a low-growing, perennial plant, also known as Lesser catmint, with an erect habit. The grayish-green, aromatic leaves have a surface coating of fine hairs and are broadly oval in shape. The flowers appear from midsummer until early autumn in a range of colours from white to lilac or pinkish-mauve. *C. n. glandulosa* 'White Cloud' has pure white flowers, and the flowers of *C. n. glandulosa* 'Blue Cloud' are bluish-mauve. Propagation is by seed, although this plant self-seeds quite freely.

Convolvulus cneorum
H 75cm (2.5ft) Zones 8-10
Silverbush is an evergreen shrub of compact and low-growing bushy habit, has silvery, silky narrow-pointed leaves on silver hairy stems, and is slightly tender, but it is a superb plant for hot, dry conditions. The flowers are a soft pink in tight buds, opening to a pure white with a small golden-yellow eye in the centre, produced at the tips of the shoots from May to September. Propagate by semi-ripe cuttings taken in summer.

Dianthus
H 40cm (16in) Zones 3-10
These attractive, sun-loving plants, better known as carnations, form sprawling, cushion-like mounds of silver-gray foliage. The silver-gray stems carry leaves that are very narrow and almost look like spikes, as they are usually pointed and often have blue or gray-green appearance. They are ideal for the front of a border or bed, as they produce flushes of delicately scented, brightly coloured blooms in colours ranging from white through many shades of pink to dark-reds in summer and again in the autumn. Propagation is by division every three years, or layering in late summer.

Erigeron karvinskianus
H 15-30cm (6-12in) Zones 5-9
This little daisy, also known as Fleabane, is a vigorous, spreading perennial that quickly forms a carpet of small lance-shaped gray-green leaves. In summer, the plant is studded with small daisy flowers that open white and age through pink to purple. It does well in between paving stones and in walls. Grow in full sun and propagate by cuttings or by sowing seed in late spring.

Erinus alpinus
H 8cm (3in) Zones 4-9
The Alpine liverwort originates from North Africa and the warmer parts of Europe and has small leaves above which rise clouds of small pink, purple, or white flowers from late spring to summer. It does best in well-drained soil in sun or partial shade, and makes a good plant for paving or on walls. You can propagate it from seed but it also self-seeds easily. It is trouble-free.

Gypsophila paniculata
H 1.2m (4ft) Zones 4-9
This herbaceous perennial, known as Baby's breath, is a traditional garden favourite, with thin strap-like gray-green leaves carried on thick gray-green stems. In summer, masses of very small white flowers are produced in large clusters, giving the appearance of a white haze over the plant. Double and pink-flowered forms are also available; *G. p.* 'Bristol Fairy', has double white blooms, *G. p.* 'Flamingo' has double pink blooms. Propagation is by root cuttings taken when the plant is dormant.

Gypsophila repens
H 20cm (8in) Zones 3-4
This pretty small perennial has narrow bluish green leaves and clouds of tiny, starry white to pinkish purple flowers for a long period in summer. It makes spreading clumps that drape effectively over path edges. This plant needs sharply drained soil and a position in full sun. Propagate from seed in a cold frame in spring. Although mainly trouble-free, it will rot if exposed to too much winter wet.

Dianthus

Lewisia
H 30cm (1ft) Zones 3-9
These beautiful, evergreen, perennial plants are grown for their colourful, funnel-shaped flowers. They produce broad flat rosettes of thick, fleshy, strap-like dark green leaves with toothed margins. The flowers are produced in shades of pink, magenta, yellow, white, and orange on slender green stems. *L. cotyledon* (zones 6-9) is well worth growing. The plants must have a free-draining soil or they will rot. Propagate by seed sown in autumn or dividing rosettes after flowering.

Linum perenne
H 45cm (18in) Zones 5-8
Perennial Flax is clump-forming, with slender stems bearing narrow, lance-shaped, bluish-green leaves. From early to midsummer, small clear-blue, funnel-shaped flowers are produced on the tips of the shoots. The individual flowers only last for one day. The cultivar *L. p.* 'Blau Saphir' is smaller than *Linum perenne* and produces vivid sky-blue flowers. Propagation is by tip cuttings taken after the flowers have faded.

Pulsatilla vulgaris
H 15-23cm (6-9in) Zones 4-9
Known as the Pasque flower because it flowers at Easter, this pretty, small perennial produces attractive, nodding, bell-shaped flowers in shades of delicate pale purple, red, pink, or white, with prominent yellow stamens. The leaves are feathery and light, being finely divided, in leaflets about 15cm (6in) long. The flower stems elongate rapidly as feathery seeds mature. It needs free-draining, gravely soil. Propagate by taking root cuttings in winter.

Sedum spectabile
H 45cm (18in) Zones 4-9
This is a clump-forming, deciduous perennial, also known as Everlasting, with thick, fleshy, broadly oval leaves, white-green in colour, and carried in pairs on thick, fleshy stems. The pink or mauve-tinged flower heads are 10cm (4in) or more wide, and appear in late summer and early autumn. 'Brilliant', is an outstanding *S. spectabile* hybrid with large, bright pink flower heads, and *S. s* 'Iceberg' has paler leaves and pure white flowers. Propagate by division.

Sempervivum
H 15cm (6in) Zones 5-10
This hardy, evergreen succulent, commonly known as Hens and chicks, has oval, fleshy leaves with pointed tips often tinted reddish-purple. They curve around each other to form tight rosettes. Each rosette produces star-like flowers in summer. A wide range of species and cultivars are available, but *S. arachnoideum* is very attractive, the tips of its leaves being woven together with a white mat of hairs, giving a cobweb appearance. Propagate by removing young rosettes.

Sisyrinchium graminoides (syn S. angustifolium)
H 50cm (20in) Zones 5-8
Known as Blue-eyed grass, this attractive clump-forming perennial looks rather like a Japanese iris, with narrow, strap-shaped semi-evergreen leaves and small, yellow-throated, blue flowers at the tips of long slender stems in summer. These are borne in succession over a long period. *S. graminoides* self-seeds freely, making it a useful contender for semi-wild gardens. Prefers poor soil and full sun and does not tolerate winter wet. Divide in spring. Generally trouble-free except in wet conditions.

Thymus doerfleri
H 15cm (6in) Zones 6-9
Thyme, a sub-shrub, has richly fragrant, tiny dark green leaves and clouds of purplish-pink flowers in midsummer. *T.d.* 'Bressingham' is smaller with pink flowers. It makes a good subject for planting in paving, as does *T. serpyllym*, all of which release their fragrance when trodden on. *T.s.* 'Snowdrift' has white flowers. Propagate from rooted stem section in summer.

Erigeron karvinskianus

Lewisia cotyledon hybrids

Linum perenne

Sempervivum

Thymus doerfleri 'Bressingham Pink'

MEDIUM PERENNIALS FOR DROUGHT

Agapanthus campanulatus
H 1m (3ft) Zones 7-10
The African blue lily is a clump-forming evergreen perennial with long, tough, gray-green strap-like leaves. The globe-shaped clusters of dark blue flowers are carried on long slender green stems from mid- to late summer. Notable forms include *A. c.* 'Albovittatus', which has a white stripe in each leaf, and *A. c. patens*, which is much smaller and has pale blue flowers. Pruning simply consists of cutting down the old flower stalks. Propagation is by division in the spring. There are a number of cultivars that tend to be hardier than the species forms. *A.* 'Blue Giant' (1.2m/4ft) is one, as is *A.* 'Snowy Owl', with white flowers.

Brachyglottis (Senecio) 'Sunshine'
H 1m (3ft) Zones 7-10
This low, spreading shrub has an open lax habit, often spreading to 3m (10ft) wide. The young leaves and stems are covered in a silvery gray felt, which gradually disappears as the shoots age. In summer, large sprays of yellow, daisy-like flowers are produced on the tips of shoots and branches. This plant should be pruned soon after flowering to prevent it becoming too straggly. Propagation is by semi-ripe cuttings taken after flowering.

Crambe cordifolia
H 2m (6ft) Zones 6-9
Colewort starts as a clump, but develops into a large, spreading plant with large kidney-shaped leaves with crinkled margins and dark green stems. Through late spring and early summer, the plant is covered with clouds of small white flowers held above the leaves on slender green stalks. Prune in the winter by cutting the stems down to soil level. Propagate by division in spring.

Cynara cardunculus
H 2m (6ft) Zones 7-9
This is a vigorous, clump-forming perennial, also known as Cardoon, with large deeply divided silvery gray leaves often tipped with sharp spines. The young stems are also silver-gray in colour, often turning green with age. Purple, thistle-like flower heads are produced on silvery, felt-covered stems from midsummer until mid-autumn. This plant is susceptible to slug damage in the spring. Propagation is by division in the spring or by root cuttings in the winter.

Echinops ritro
H 60cm (2ft) Zones 3-9
The Small globe thistle is a clump-forming herbaceous perennial with a compact habit and sturdy stems. The stiff spiny leaves are deeply cut and dark green with a thin spider's web-like felt over the upper surface and a white down beneath. The young stems are also gray-green in colour. In late summer, the flowers consist of tight metallic blue globes about 5cm (2in) across. The cultivar *E. r.* 'Veitch's Blue' is a darker blue . Propagation is by root cuttings or division in spring.

Eryngium bourgatii
H 75cm (2.5ft) Zones 5-9
This clump-forming herbaceous perennial, known also as Sea holly, has tough, prickly leaves that vary in colour from silvery gray to gray-green, with the stems showing the same variations in colour. In summer and autumn, tufted globes of metallic gray blue flowers, each surrounded by a ruff of leathery spines are produced on the shoot tips, the dead flowers often lasting well into the winter. Propagate by root cuttings or division in the spring. This plant may be slow to establish.

Lavandula
H 30-120cm (1-4ft) Zones 5-10
These evergreen, mainly summer-flowering shrubs are grown for their aromatic foliage and flowers, and often make effective low hedges. Leaves are gray-green, either entire or divided. Lavender needs a sunny position. Popular cultivars are *L.* 'Hidcote' , which produces dense spikes of fragrant deep purple flowers from mid- to late summer, and *L. stoechas,* or French lavender, which bears heads of tiny purple flowers topped by rose-purple bracts, in summer. Propagate by semi-ripe cuttings in summer.

Phlomis fruticosa
H 1m (3ft) Zones 7-9
The Jerusalem sage is an attractive shrub that forms a dense evergreen mound of thin, straggly branches with oval gray-green, deeply veined, sage-like leaves and

Agapanthus 'Blue Giant'

Crambe cordifolia

Cynara cardunculus

Lavandula stoechas

Salvia patens

Verbascum phoeniceum

gray-green stems with a felty coating over the surface, which disappears as they age. The bright yellow, large, deadnettle-like flowers are produced in large circular trusses on the tops of the stems. In spring, prune back the shoots by approximately one-third to prevent the plant becoming too straggly. Propagation is by cuttings taken in late summer.

Rosmarinus officinalis

H 2m (6ft) Zones 8-10

An attractive aromatic shrub, Rosemary forms an open, evergreen mound of thin straggly branches with narrow leaves, dark green in colour on the upper side, paler beneath. The light blue, tubular flowers emerge in small clusters from the leaf joints in spring and summer. Other cultivars include; *R. o.* 'Roseus' which has pink flowers and *R. o.* 'Tuscan Blue', which has dark blue flowers. This plant dislikes hard pruning, but it can be tipped regularly. Propagation is by semi-ripe cuttings taken in late summer and early autumn.

Salvia patens

H 45-60cm (18-24in) Zones 8-9

Gentian sage is a handsome perennial with bright green, slightly hairy, long spear-shaped leaves. It bears attractive spires of deep blue flowers during summer. *S.p.* 'Cambridge Blue' has paler blue flowers. *S. patens* grows well in moist soil in full sun or light shade. Propagate by division or softwood cuttings in early summer. This plant is prone to attack from slugs and snails.

Santolina chamaecyparissus

H 60cm (2ft) Zones 6-9

Lavender cotton is a compact, mound-shaped shrub spreading to 1m (3ft) across. The narrow, aromatic leaves are silver-gray and covered in a fine felt covering, which also covers the young shoots and stems. From mid- to late summer, bright yellow flowerheads are carried above the leaves on slender gray stems. *S. c.* 'Pretty Carol' is a lower-growing cultivar with soft gray leaves. Propagation is by semi-ripe cuttings taken in late summer and early autumn.

Sedum spectabile

H 45cm (18in) Zones 4-9

Sometimes known as Ice plant or Stonecrop, this deciduous herbaceous perennial produces broad, flat clusters of star-shaped pink flowers in late summer on thick gray-green stalks. The plant forms a dense clump of thick, fleshy gray-green leaves carried on erect stems from mid-spring onwards. *S. s.* 'Brilliant', has deep pink flowers, while those of *S. s.* 'Iceberg', are pure white. All are very attractive to bees. Prune off dead flower heads in spring. Propagate by division in spring.

Silene uniflora 'Flore Pleno'

H 15cm (6in) Zones 3-7

This small, creeping, semi-evergreen perennial, also known as the Double sea campion or Catchfly, has lax wandering roots. The leaves are grayish-green in colour and lance-shaped, while taller branching stems produce pom-pom-like double white flowers during summer. The

small campions do best in alpine-type conditions, but the bigger ones will tolerate light shade. Propagate from basal cuttings in spring. Can be attractive to slugs and snails.

Stachys byzantina

H 40cm (16in) Zones 4-8

Also known as Bunnies' ears, or Lamb's tongue, this low-growing perennial is one of the most useful plants for growing in light soils and sunny positions, spreading over the ground. Its evergreen leaves and stems are covered with fine silvery hairs, making them look woolly and silvery gray especially in bright sunlight. It is useful at the front of a border or as ground cover. *S. b.* 'Silver Carpet' has very silvery foliage. Fluffy spikes of small mauve flowers are produced in summer. This plant likes a sunny position and well-drained soil. Propagate by removing self-layered shoots in the spring.

Verbascum phoeniceum

H 1.2m (4ft) Zones 4-8

Purple mullein is an evergreen herbaceous perennial which forms a flat rosette of deeply veined, oval-shaped, dark green leaves with crinkled margins for most of the year. In the late spring and early summer, a tall, almost leafless, flower spike emerges before flowers are produced. The flowers are highly variable in colour, ranging from white to pink to dark purple, and open from the base up to the tip of the stem. Propagation is by division in late spring or root cuttings in winter.

BULBS

Allium
H 75cm (30in)

These ornamental onions are summer-flowering bulbs, often with globe-like flower heads made up of many small individual flowers. These can vary in colour from white to deep pinks, purple, or blue, and in the case of *A. moly* (zones 7-9), golden yellow. The narrow strap-like leaves are usually dark green, as are the flower stalks. These plants prefer a well-drained soil and are propagated by seed or division in autumn or spring. *A. karataviense* (zones 3-9) has very attractive, large, grayish-green, flattish leaves and typical allium-like heads of starry pink flowers in summer.

Anemone blanda
H 15cm (6in) Zones 4-8

The Grecian windflower is a vigorous, clump-forming perennial with a low-growing, creeping habit. The dark green leaves are deeply lobed and carried above the ground on thin, wiry, dark or bluish-green stems. In spring, single flowers in shades of white, pink, and deep blue are carried above the leaves. Notable cultivars include; *A. b.* 'Ingramii', which has deep blue flowers with a purple reverse, and *A. b.* 'White Splendour', which is pure white. Propagation is by division after flowering.

Convallaria majalis
H 25cm (10in) Zones 2-8

The lily-of-the-valley is a tough perennial with a creeping habit and is ideal for a shaded spot. The broadly lance-shaped leaves are deep green and usually arranged in pairs. Clusters of pure white, heavily scented, bell-like flowers appear in late spring, held on dark green stems above the ground. There is a variegated cultivar; *C. m.* 'Albostriata' with cream and green striped leaves, and *C. m.* var. *rosea* has pink flowers. Propagation is by division in the autumn.

Crocus
H 15cm (6in) Zones 3-8

There are a good many species in this genus. For planting in grass, choose the more vigorous forms such as *C. speciosus*, a autumn-flowering crocus, and *C. vernus* (the Dutch crocus), which has white, lilac or purple flowers in spring to early summer. There are many varieties of both species; those of *C. vernus* sometimes have striped flowers. Plant in poor soil in full sun.

Cyclamen
H 5-20cm (2-8in) Zones 5-9

Hardy cyclamen are incredibly tough little perennial plants, with almost-round leaves held up on curling red stems. Many species have pronounced silver markings on their dark green leaves. *C. coum* reaches only 8cm (3in) high and produces delicate flowers in shades of pink through to carmine-red in late winter or early spring, while *C. hederifolium* grows up to 12cm (5in) and bears pink flowers with maroon markings in autumn. Propagation is by seed sown as soon as it is ripe.

Eranthus hyemalis
H 10cm (4in) Zones 4-9

Winter aconite is a tuberous-rooted, hardy perennial valued because it flowers so early. In early spring, this plant produces small, buttercup-like yellow flowers on a collar of pale-green, deeply cut leaves, carried on short, greenish-brown stems. This is a perfect plant for naturalizing in a woodland setting or under large shrubs. Propagate by division in spring immediately after the flowers have died down, but replant them immediately.

Erythronium
H 20cm (8in) Zones 3-9

Also known as Dog's tooth violet or Trout lily, these attractive perennial bulbs have broad, strap-shaped leaves of a lush deep green with greenish brown markings. Small, lily-like flowers are carried on slender green or purple-green stems in spring. *E. dens-canis* carries solitary white, pink or purple flowers on 15cm (6in) stems, while *E. revolutum* produces up to four yellow-centreed lilac flowers on each stem. These plants may need protection from slugs in the spring. Propagate by division after flowering.

Fritillaria imperialis
H 1.5m (5ft) Zones 5-9

The Crown Imperial is a handsome bulbous perennial that has striking hanging clusters of burnt orange flowers surmounted by a 'crown' of leaflike bracts (hence the

Allium karavatiense

Eranthis hyemalis

Fritillaria imperialis

common name) in late spring/early summer. Does best in fertile soil in full sun. Plant the bulbs at a depth of four times their length, on their sides. *F. imperialis* bulbs will rot in poorly drained soil. Divide offsets to propagate. Generally trouble-free, but prone to slug and lily beetle attacks.

Galanthus nivalis

H 10-15cm (4-6in) Zones 3-9
The Common snowdrop is a hardy, clump-forming, low-growing bulb. It has flat, strap-shaped leaves arranged in pairs, usually one on either side of the flower stalk. They are a dull mid-green or bluish-green. Grown for its white flowers produced in the early spring, there are several popular cultivars and species; *G. n.* 'Flore Pleno' has double white flowers. An attractive species for the garden is *G. elwesii*, which is larger and more vigorous with larger flowers flecked green in spring. Propagation is by division immediately after flowering.

Leucojum aestivum

H 60cm (2ft) Zones 4-9
Called the Summer snowflake, this bulbous plant is a close relative of the snowdrop. It has dark-green, strap-like leaves up to 40cm (16in) long. In the spring, up to eight bell-shaped white flowers are produced on each green stem. The cultivar *L. a.* 'Gravetye Giant' produces larger, green-tipped white flowers and grows up to 90cm (3ft) tall. Propagate by removing offsets from the base of the bulb once the leaves have died down.

Lilium

H 1m (3ft) Zones 2-9
Lilies have bold, shapely, trumpet-like, often very fragrant blooms made up of six petals that develop into an open star shape that can vary in size from 2.5cm (1in) to 25cm (10in) across, depending upon the variety. The leaves are pale to dark green; some are narrow, almost grass-like and grouped at the base of the plant, while others produce leaves in clusters (whorls) at intervals along the stems, topped by flowers from early summer to late autumn, according to variety. Propagate from scales in September and October. *L. regale* produces highly scented, typical lily flowers in summer. This plant prefers alkaline soil and full sun.

Muscari armeniacum

H 38cm (15in) Zones 4-8
The Grape hyacinth is a hardy, dwarf bulbous plant with thin green leaves that spread and separate as the flowers appear. The flower heads are compact and densely packed, to form a tight spike of deep blue

flowers with white rims, produced in late spring. There are also some distinct named varieties, such as *M. a.* 'Cantab', which is paler blue, and *M. a.* 'Heavenly Blue', which is a much brighter blue. Propagate by division in midsummer.

Narcissus

H 8-50cm (3-20in) Zones 3-9
Daffodils are hardy, perennial, spring-flowering bulbs with narrow strap-like mid- to dark-green leaves, usually in groups of three or five. Each flower has an inner trumpet or cup, and an outer row of petals. The dwarf cultivar 'Tête-à-tête' is only 15cm (6in) tall and has broad yellow petals. *N. papyraceus* ('Paper White'), is heavily scented. Propagate by division when the bulbs are lifted after flowering. *N.* 'Peeping Tom' is small (15cm/6in) with bright yellow flowers with long trumpets.

Scilla siberica

H 10-15cm (4-6in) Zones 2-8
Known as the Siberian squill, this pretty bulb has slender fleshy leaves and many drooping bright blue flowers in spring. *S.s.* 'Alba' has snow white flowers; 'Spring Beauty' very bright blue ones. Plant in autumn in good soil in sun or partial shade. Can be prone to virus diseases. Pot offsets to propagate.

Tulipa

H up to 60cm (2ft) Zones 3-8
Tulips are hardy, perennial, spring-flowering bulbs with broadly oval strap-like mid- to dark green leaves, often fixed to the base of the green flower stem. They are classified and grouped according to their botanical origins and their time of flowering, with a vast range of colours from pure white through yellows, pinks and reds to almost-black. The low-growing *T. kaufmanniana* hybrids are particularly popular because they only grow to about 20cm (8in) high and require very little attention. Propagate by division after flowering.

Galanthus nivalis

Lilium regale

Muscari armeniacum

Narcissus 'Peeping Tom'

PLANTS FOR DAMP AND WATER

Aponogeton distachyos

H 5cm (2in) Zones 3-10
The Water hawthorn is so hardy that it often keeps its oblong-shaped, mid-green leaves with maroon markings throughout a temperate winter. Seen floating just above the water's surface, white blossoms are forked with two rows of black stamens at their base, and are produced from mid-spring until late autumn. The growth arises from a tuber that is almost impossible to divide individually, so propagation is usually either by division of clumps during the growing season, or by seed sown as soon as it is ready.

Aruncus dioicus

H 2m (6ft) Zones 3-9
This big tough perennial, also known as Goatsbeard, has long, fern-like leaves and loose pyramids of creamy white flowers in summer. *A.d.* 'Kneiffii' has more delicate flowers on arching stems. Plant in moist soil in full or partial shade. Divide in spring or autumn.

Astilbe × arendsii

H 1m (3ft) Zones 4-8
This stunning garden herbaceous perennial has deep green, finely-cut, fern-like foliage, carried on thin, wiry, reddish-green stems. Some of the red-flowered cultivars have bronze-tipped young foliage in the spring. In midsummer, large pointed spikes of colourful plume-like blooms form, which remain attractive even when the flowers die. A large number of cultivars are now available : *A.* × *a.* 'Snowdrift' has creamy white spikes and *A.* × *a.* 'Fever' has salmon-red blooms. Propagate by division in autumn.

Caltha palustris

H 30-60cm (1-2ft) Zones 3-7
The Marsh marigold is one of the loveliest spring-flowering marginal aquatic plants, with its bright golden-yellow, open saucer-shaped flowers held just above the leaves. This deciduous herbaceous perennial has mounds of dark green glossy foliage. There is a double-flowered cultivar *C. p.* 'Flore Pleno', and a white-flowered form *C. p.* var. *alba*. Propagation is by seed sown as soon as it has ripened in the summer, or by division immediately after flowering has finished.

Hosta sieboldiana

H 60cm (2ft) Zones 3-9
The Plantain lily is one of the most beautiful herbaceous perennials, with small, trumpet-like pendulous flowers carried on tall green stems above the leaves from midsummer. These plants are grown for their attractive foliage (which is very prone to slug damage). Leaf shapes range from long and narrow through to oval with a pointed tip. Colours vary from blue to rich combinations of silver or golden variegations. *H.* 'Gold Standard', has broadly spear-shaped gold leaves, each with a delicate dark green margin, and soft lilac-blue flowers. Propagation is by division in early spring.

Iris ensata

H 90cm (36in) Zones 5-8
This Japanese iris, from the *laevigatae* group, thrives in damp places, such as the margins of ponds or stream banks. The flowers are beardless and slightly flattened; the species is purple-flowered, but cultivars exist in a range of colours: 'Alba' is pure white; 'Blue Peter' is bright blue. Divide clumps in early autumn to propagate.

Ligularia dentata 'Desdemona'

H 1.2m (4ft) Zones 4-8
Golden groundsel is a very attractive member of the daisy family with big, bright orange daisy flowers that appear in late summer carried on tall, orange-brown stems. This herbaceous perennial produces heart-shaped, deep green leaves with an orange-red underside, in complete

Aruncus diocius

Astilbe x arendsii

contrast to the flowers. It prefers a sunny site, but the soil must be kept moist. Unfortunately, the young growths are often damaged by slugs. Propagation is by division in the spring.

Lobelia cardinalis

H 75cm (30in) Zones 5-8

This is a hardy perennial clump-forming plant with an erect, upright habit, which spreads through the soil by means of rhizomes. The stems are often reddish-purple in colour, and carry spear-shaped green leaves, which often have a bronze-purple tinge to the margins. From late summer, long spikes of cardinal red flowers are produced on the tips of the shoots. There are also white and pink flowered forms of this plant available. Propagate by division or softwood cuttings in the spring.

Mimulus luteus

H 60cm (2ft) Zones 4-7

Commonly known as the Yellow monkey flower, this plant produces golden-yellow trumpets with a narrow base mottled red on the inside, from midsummer until mid-autumn. This is an herbaceous perennial with mid-green glossy leaves arranged on thick fleshy stems that spread and root as they grow. A second flush of blooms can be encouraged by cutting down the stems immediately after flowering. Propagation is by seed sown in the spring.

Nymphaea

H 10cm (4in)

The Waterlily is truly the queen of aquatic plants. These deciduous herbaceous perennials need deep (1m/3ft) still water. They produce dark green, often bronze-tinted, circular floating leaves in spring. These are later followed by open flowers that look like floating stars, with colours ranging from pure white to shades of yellow and deeper pinks, oranges, and reds, depending on the cultivar. *N. tetragona* (zones 7-10) is the tiniest water lily, with white flowers 2-3cm (1in) across. Propagation is by division in the spring.

Peltiphyllum peltatum syn. Darmera peltata

H 1.2m (4ft) Zones 5-9

The Japanese knotweed is a spreading herbaceous perennial has large, rounded mid-green, disc-shaped leaves carried on long slender leaf-stalks. In autumn, these leaves turn an interesting bronze-pink. In spring, pale pink flowers with a white reverse to the petals are carried in large, round clusters on dark greenish-brown stems, covered in fine white hairs. The

flowers and stems appear before the leaves have emerged. Propagation is by division of the rhizomes in the spring.

Primula pulverulenta

H 1m (3ft) Zones 5-9

The se rosette-forming primulas, known as Candelabra primulas, naturalize well in moist soil. From the centre of their rosettes of leaves rise flower spikes of rose-purple tubular flowers in late spring and early summer. *P.p.* 'Bartley' has pink flowers with a red centre. *P. japonica* (the Japanese primrose) is similar but smaller. This plant grows best in partial shade in moist soil. Propagate from seed in early spring or divide in late autumn.

Pulmonaria officinalis

H 25cm (10in) Zones 4-8

Known as Jerusalem cowslip, or Soldiers and sailors, this clump-forming evergreen perennial has long, spotted leaves and whitish-blue, funnel-shaped flowers in spring. It needs damp, but not waterlogged, conditions and makes good ground cover. *P.* 'Sissinghurst White' has pure white flowers. Propagate by division in autumn.

Ranunculus aquatilis

H 10cm (4in) Zones 5-8

Water crowfoot is one of the finest of the hardy submerged aquatics. With a scattering of attractive floating dark-green foliage that looks rather like clover leaves; also there are impressive underwater leaves made from thin filaments. The slender green stems can run for several metres through the water. In midsummer, glistening delicate white and gold flowers are produced just above the surface of the water. Propagation is by cuttings taken from the underwater parts of the plant in spring.

Typha minima

H 45cm (18in) Zones 3-11

The Dwarf cattail is a delicate-looking little plant and, unlike many of its larger relatives, is not at all invasive, making it perfect for a smaller garden where it will grow well in shallow water. The long, slender, dark green, 'grass-like' leaves are followed by chunky, brown flowering heads that are almost circular in shape, and which last well into the winter. These smaller 'bullrush' flower heads are much favored by flower arrangers. Propagation is by division in the early spring, just as the leaves emerge.

Zantedeschia aethiopica

H 1m (3ft) Zones 8-10

This herbaceous perennial, also known as the Calla lily, has a thick, fleshy rootstock producing broad, spear-shaped deep green

leaves, and thrives in moist soil or shallow water. In summer, the large white lopsided flowers, borne on green stems, have a golden yellow spike in the centre. There is a superior cultivar, *Z. a.* 'Crowborough', which is hardier, more compact, and produces more flowers. Propagation is by division in the early spring. These plants may suffer aphid damage in dry periods.

EASY-CARE TIP

When clearing weeds from a pond, always leave it on the edge of the pond overnight. This will allow any snails, frogs or insects to crawl back into the pond so that the natural balance within the pond is not upset.

Iris ensata

Ligularia dentata 'Desdemona'

FERNS

FERNS THAT TOLERATE SHADE

Adiantum pedatum

H 30 cm (1ft) Zones 3-8

The deciduous American maidenhair fern is low-growing with pale green fronds, almost triangular in shape, held erect on stiff bluish-black stems. *A. aleuticum*, a relative, is slightly taller and the new fronds are often tinged with pink in spring. Propagate by division in spring, or by sowing spores.

Athyrium filix-femina

H 50cm (20in) Zones 4-9

This deciduous fern has finely cut, pale green, lance-shaped fronds that die down in winter to expose the central crown of the plant. These plants will tolerate lime, but prefer an acid soil. Propagate by sowing spores, or by division in the spring.

Blechnum spicant

H 45cm (18in) Zones 4-8

The evergreen Deer fern is low-growing with a creeping, spreading habit. The glossy, dark-green, deeply cut leaves are arranged in tight rosettes. It is easy to grow in full or partial shade, especially on an acid, moist but well-drained soil. Propagate by division in the spring, or by sowing spores, but it is slow to establish after dividing.

Dicksonia antarctica

H 2.5m (8ft) Zones 9-10

The tree fern is a distinctive plant with huge, spreading, deeply cut fronds, often producing a canopy of mid-green leaves. The dark brown 'stem' is actually a mass of root fibers and old leaf stalks that can reach up to 6m (20ft) in height. Propagate by sowing spores, but plants are very slow to mature.

Dryopteris filix-mas

H 1.2m (4ft) Zones 4-8

The Male fern is a deciduous or sometimes semi-evergreen fern that thrives in shade but is able to tolerate some bright sunlight. As it grows, it forms a clump of lance-shaped, deeply cut fronds. *D. f-m.* 'Grandiceps Wills' has a broad heavy crest at the tip of each frond, making it a truly striking plant. Propagate by division in the spring, or by sowing spores as soon as they are ripe.

Matteucia struthiopteris

H 1m (3ft) Zones 2-8

The Shuttlecock fern or Ostrich fern is a deciduous plant grown for its attractive leaves. It has an outer rim of elegant, pale yellow-green, gently-arching fronds (leaves) and the inner fronds are shorter and dark greenish-brown. The fronds are extremely thin, with a blackish-brown middle rib. It needs a damp, well-drained soil. Propagate by division in late-spring.

FERNS THAT TOLERATE SUN

Asplenium scolopendrium

H 60cm (2ft) Zones 4-8

The evergreen Hart's tongue fern produces shuttlecock-like crowns of broad curling strap-like leaves, which are a bright glossy green in colour with a thick greenish brown rib running down the centre. One very striking cultivar is *A. s.* 'Crispum', which is grown for its mid-green fronds which have very wavy, crested margins to the leaves. Propagate by division in the spring, or by sowing spores in the spring.

Cyrtomium falcatum

H 60cm (2ft) Zones 7-9

A fern which looks more like a holly bush, hence its common name of Japanese holly fern. This evergreen plant prefers a damp, free-draining soil, grows from an erect 'stock' or rhizome, and has a spreading habit. An interesting cultivar is *C. f.* 'Cristatum', with heavily divided and crested tips to the fronds. Propagation where possible is by sowing spores in late summer.

Onoclea sensibilis

H 1m (3ft) Zones 4-8

The Sensitive fern is a deciduous plant that produces upright, later arching fronds, almost triangular in shape. The new fronds in spring boast attractive pinkish bronze tints. This plant prefers a little dappled shade, as the fronds may burn if exposed to scorching sun. Propagate by division in the spring, or by sowing spores as soon as they are ripe.

Osmunda regalis

H 1.2m (4ft) Zones 3-9

The Royal fern is deciduous, very attractive, and grows to form a dense clump with large pale green fronds that start by growing very upright before gently arching over towards the ground. This plant thrives in a damp soil close to a pond or stream. Pruning consists of cutting away the old dead fronds in late spring. Propagate by division in spring.

Polypodium vulgare

H 40cm (16in) Zones 5-8

This low-growing evergreen fern, also known as the Wall polypody, has deeply cut, dark green leaves with a tough leathery texture. The plant has a low spreading habit, often creeping over the ground as rhizomes. It prefers a free-draining site. Propagate by division in spring or early summer.

Polystichum setiferum

H 1m (3ft) 5-8

Also called the Soft shield fern or Hedge fern, this moisture-loving plant is grown for its attractive evergreen foliage. The mid-green coloured, soft-textured fronds are finely divided into lots of segments, and arranged in a clump to resemble the flights of a shuttlecock. Propagate by division in spring.

Dryopteris filix-mas

Osmunda regalis

EDIBLE PLANTS

Alpine strawberry (*Fragaria vesca* 'Semperflorens')

H 15cm (6in) Zones 4-9
This low-growing, evergreen herbaceous perennial produces clusters of small white flowers in late spring and early summer, followed by small, edible fragrant strawberries until midsummer. This plant also makes excellent ground cover, but the plants need to be replaced every three years or so. Propagate by seed sown in spring.

Broad beans (*Vicia faba*)

H 1m (3ft) Zones 7-10
This is one of the easiest vegetables to grow, as well as being one of the earliest to mature, producing white flowers with black markings from early to mid-summer. The green seeds are edible and each plant will produce about 150g (5oz) of food. Propagate by seed sown in autumn or spring.

Chinese cabbage (*Brassica rapa*)

H 60cm (2ft) Zones 7-10
This is a fast-growing vegetable that looks rather like a hybrid between cabbage and lettuce. The loose-headed cultivars are popular, as the outer leaves can be harvested continually. The plants will usually reach maturity 10-12 weeks after sowing. Propagate by seed in spring and summer.

Chives (*Allium schoenoprasum*)

H 45cm (18in) Zones 4-9
This deciduous herbaceous perennial is a close relative of the onion, and is an ideal 'starter' plant for the beginner or busy gardener, as it will tolerate almost total neglect. In summer, compact globes of small, pale-purple flowers are produced on the tips of shoots. The leaves are used as flavoring for soups, salads, cheese dishes, and omelettes. Propagate by division in autumn or spring.

Lettuce (*Lactuca sativa*)

H 30cm (1ft) Zones 7-10
This annual plant is grown for its crisp, edible leaves and has bewildering number of cultivars with varied leaf shapes and types with colours ranging from pale green through to greenish-purple. Crinkle-leaved cultivars, such as 'Salad Bowl', and 'Lollo Rosso' are particularly popular as they can be harvested by continually removing the outer leaves as the plant continues to develop. Propagation is by seed.

Mint (*Mentha spicata*)

H 45cm (18in) Zones 3-10
The spearmint is a deciduous herbaceous perennial that produces spikes of small, pinky-blue flowers in midsummer. It is ideal as a flavoring for mint sauce or boiled with potatoes as a flavoring. This plant should be grown in a container as it can be very invasive. Propagate by division in autumn or spring.

Oregano (*Origanum vulgare*)

H 30cm (1ft) Zones 5-9
This low, spreading plant has rounded aromatic dark green leaves and produces clusters of deep pink to white-flushed pink flowers from midsummer to early autumn. The leaves are used as flavoring for a variety of dishes. Propagate by cuttings taken in spring.

Radish (*Raphanus sativus*)

H 10-15cm (4-6in) Zones 6-10
This hardy annual is quick and easy to grow, often reaching maturity within 5-8 weeks of sowing the seed. As the plant matures, the fiery-flavoured, edible red root swells. Green, yellow, and blackish-purple skinned cultivars are available. Propagation is by seed sown in spring and summer.

Rhubarb (*Rheum × cultorum*)

H 75cm (30in) Zones 3-9
Eaten as a fruit, this long-lived hardy herbaceous perennial is actually a vegetable, producing pinky-red leaf stalks in late spring to midsummer. Once established, a plant will crop for 10-15 years, with little care or attention other than removal of flowers as they emerge in summer. Propagate by division in late autumn.

Rocket (*Eruca versicaria sativa*)

H 45cm (18in) Zones 7-10
This plant is grown for salads, as its leaves have a hot savory flavour. It will stand repeated cutting throughout the growing season, and can grow outdoors through the average winter. Propagation is by seed sown outdoors in the spring.

Common sage (*Salvia officinalis*)

H 60cm (24in) Zones 6-9
This herb is easy to grow in full sun or light shade and dryish soil. The grayish-green leaves are very aromatic. Small blue flowers are borne in early to midsummer. *S.o.* 'Purpurascens' has attractive, purple-flushed young leaves. Propagate from semi-ripe cuttings in late summer.

Mentha x piperata

Rocket (*Eruca versicaria sativa*)

Salvia officinalis 'Purpurascens'

INDEX

A

Abies koreana 66, 118
Acanthus spinosus 128, *128*
Acer 70, *71*
    A. griseum 33, 66
    A. japonicum dissectum 70
    A. palmatum 79, 93
    A. pseudoplatanus 79
Achillea millefolium 40, *42*, 75
Acorus gramineus 79
Adiantum pedatum 138
African blue lily 132
Agapanthus 49
    A. 'Blue Giant' 60, *61*, 132, *132*
    A. campanulatus 132
Agave 48, *48*, 49
Agrimonia eupatoria 75
Agrostis 37
Ajuga reptans 79, 80, 124
Alchemilla mollis 12, 49, 60, 93, 122, *122*
Algerian iris 128
Allium 134, *134*
    A. schoenoprasum 139
alpine liverwort 130
alpine strawberry 139
alpines 44, 45, *48*
Alyssum spinosum 130, *130*
Amelanchier 107
Anchusa azurea 93
Anemone
    A. blanda 134
    A. nemorosa 33
angel's fishing rod 128
Anthemis 93, 122
antirrhinum *44*
aphids 113
Aponogeton distachyos 136
aquatic and damp-loving plants 136-7
Aquilegia vulgaris 93
Aralia elata 79
Argyranthemum 40, 80
Aristolochia macrophylla 79
Armeria maritima 130, *130*
Aronia 93
Artemisia 40, 49, 122
    A. absinthium 72, 75
    A. 'Powis Castle' 122, *122*
Aruncus 42
    A. dioicus (goatsbeard) 136, *136*
Arundo donax 126
Asperula odoratum 33
Asplenium scolopendrium 138
Aster umbellatus 75
Astilbe 42

A. x *arendsii* 136, *136*
Athyrium filix-femina 47, 138
Aucuba 93
    A. japonica 118
aven 128, *128*
azalea 20

B

baby's breath *see Gypsophila*
baby's tears 12, *13*, 79, 80
bamboo 66
barberry *see Berberis*
bark chippings 100, 101
barrenwort *see Epimedium grandiflorum*
bear's breeches 128, *128*
bellflower *see Campanula*
Berberis 25, *25*, 66, 78, 107
    B. x *stenophylla* 66, 118, *118*, 119
    B. thunbergii 79
Bergenia 93
    B. cordifolia 122
    B. crassifolia 122, *122*
Betula 82
    B. utilis 116
birch *see Betula*
Blechnum spicant 138
bleeding heart 128
blue fescue 126
blue oat grass 127
blue-eyed grass 131
bog gardens 26
borders
    shrub borders 38-9, *38*
    simplifying 60-1
Boston ivy 121
boundaries 24-5, *24*, *25*
    see also fences; hedges; walls
Bowles' golden sedge 126
box *see Buxus sempervirens*
Brachyglottis 93, 132
Brassica rapa 139
Briza media 126
broad beans 139
broom 45
Brugmansia 76
Brunnera 49, 82
    B. macrophylla 93, *93*, 124, *124*
Buddleja 79, 93
    B. alternifolia 107
    B. davidii 107
    B. globosa 107
bugle *see Ajuga reptans*
bulbs 105, 134-5
bulrush 84
bunnies' ears 133

buttonweed 103
Buxus sempervirens (boxwood) 24, 56, 64, 66, *66*, 68, 80, 82, *85*, *87*, 105, 111, 118, *118*, 119
buying plants 92

C

Calamagrostis x *acutiflora* 35, 126, *126*
Calamintha nepeta 130
Californian poppy *41*
calla lily 137
Calluna 93
Caltha palustris 136
Camellia 107
    C. japonica 93
Campanula 60, 93
    C. carpatica 124
Campsis x *tagliabuana* 120, *120*
candelabra primula 8, 137
Caragana arborescens 116, *116*
cardoon *see Cynara cardunculus*
Carex
    C. elata 'Aurea' 126
    C. hachijoensis 79
    C. pendula 126
carnation *see Dianthus*
Carpinus 119
Catalpa bignonioides 66
catchfly 133
catmint 74, 130
Centaurea cyanus 40
Centranthus 93
Cephalaria gigantea 75
Cercidiphyllum japonicum 93
Chaenomeles 93, 107
Chamaemelum nobile 80, 103, *103*, *104*
chamomile *see Chamaemelum nobile*
Chilean potato vine 121
Chinese cabbage 139
Chinese lantern 129
chives 139
Choisya ternata 66, 118, *118*
Cirsium heterophyllum 75
Cistus 49, 93
Clematis 107
    C. 'Jackmanii Superba' 120
    C. montana 76, 79, 120, *120*
    C. viticella 40
climbing plants 24, 120-1
    self-clinging 82
    tying in 108-9, *108*
Cobaea scandens 79
colewort 132, *132*
Colorado spruce *see Picea pungens*

common quaking grass 126
companion planting 112
containers 8
    drought-resistant plants 48-9, *48*, *49*
    feeding 95
    moving heavy containers 109, *109*
    watering 99
Convallaria majalis 134
Convolvulus 103
    C. cneorum 130
coral flower *see Heuchera*
coral spot 113, *113*
Cordyline 48, 60, 76, 78
    C. australis 78, 79
Coreopsis tripteris 42
cornflower 40
Cornus 38
    C. kousa 93
Coronilla 93
Corsican mint 103
Cortaderia selloana 35, 126, *126*
Corylus 93, 107
cosmos 44
Cotinus coggygria 66, 116, *116*
cottage garden planting 40-1, *40*, *41*, *55*
country garden 84-8, *84-8*
courtyard gardens 17, *17*, 28, *55*
crab apple 39
Crambe cordifolia 132, *132*
Crataegus 39, 80, 116, *117*
crimson flag 129
Crocosmia 40
    C. 'Emily Mackenzie' *42*
    C. 'Lucifer' *33*
    C. 'Solfaterre' *34*
Crocus 134
crown imperial 134-5, *134*
Cupressus sempervirens 66
currant, flowering *see Ribes*
cuttings 104-5, *104*
Cyclamen 134
Cynara cardunculus 87, 132, *132*
Cynodon dactylon 37
Cyperus papyrus 87
Cyrtomium falcatum 138
Cytisus 93
    C. battandieri 45, 120

D

daffodil 135, *135*
daisy 49, 74
damping-off 113
datura 76
Daucus carota 75
deadnettle *see Lamium*

ACKNOWLEDGEMENTS

We would like to thank the following for their help in producing this book. Firstly, Mandy Lebentz and Roger Daniels for their editorial and design work respectively, to Tony Lord for consultancy work and to Kate Kirby and her assistant Loryn Birkholtz for their support at Collins & Brown, and to Sorcha Hitchcox for her general editorial assistance. Steven Wooster, Andrew Lawson, Mike Paul, Clive Nichols and Henk Dijkmann in particular for their photography and Judy Dod at Andrew Lawson's Picture Library and Andrew Lord at the Garden Picture Library for their picture research. Also all the garden owners and garden designers whose work appears in this book, but particularly to owners/designers Ian Sidaway and Anthony Paul in the UK, Henk Gerritsen and Henk Weijers in Holland, Sonny Garcia in California, and to the Garretts and Clarksons in New Zealand. We would also like to thank Yvonne Innes for her border plans on pages 60-61.

Index compiled by Marie Lorimer

A few of the gardens in this book, both in the UK and abroad, can be visited by the public. To obtain information, please write to the publisher.

Illustrations:
All by Ian Sidaway, except p61 TR by Vanessa Luff

HARDINESS ZONES

The plants in the A-Z Directory are all given hardiness zones. These are an approximate guide only as to the minimum and maximum temperatures they are likely to tolerate, but wet autumns, for example, can make plants less frost-tolerant than they might normally be.

Zones	° Fahrenheit	° Celsius
Zone 1	Below -50	Below -45
Zone 2	-50 to -40	-45 to -40
Zone 3	-40 to -30	-40 to -34
Zone 4	-30 to -20	-34 to -29
Zone 5	-20 to -10	-29 to -23
Zone 6	-10 to 0	-23 to -18
Zone 7	0 to 10	-18 to -12
Zone 8	10 to 20	-12 to -7
Zone 9	20 to 30	-7 to -1
Zone 10	30 to 40	-1 to 4
Zone 11	Above 40	Above 4

PHOTOGRAPHY CREDITS

(Key: T: top; R: right; L: left; B: bottom; C: centre)
1 Steven Wooster; 2 Steven Wooster (design: Anthony Paul); 6 Steven Wooster; 7 GPL/Mike Paul; 8-9 Steven Wooster; l0 GPL/Ron Sutherland; l4 TR GPL/Jacqui Hurst; C GPL/Ron Sutherland; l5 GPL/Ron Sutherland; l6-l7 Andrew Lawson; l8-l9 Steven Wooster; 20 Steven Wooster (design; Hamish Lane/Pierce Landscape Co.); 2l Andrew Lawson/Andy Rees; 22 TL Steven Wooster; C GPL/J.S.Sira; 23 Andrew Lawson; 24 TL Steven Wooster (design: Clarkson); B Andrew Lawson; 25 T GPL/Mayer; Le Scanff; BL Steven Wooster (design: Living Earth Co) BR Andrew Lawson; 26 Steven Wooster (design: Henk Weijers); 27 Steven Wooster (design Anthony Paul); 28 GPL/Mark Bolton; C Steven Wooster/GPL; 29 GPL (TR: Ron Sutherland; C Jacqui Hurst; B Sunniva Harte); 3l Steven Wooster; 34 T GPL/Howard Rice; B Steven Wooster (design: Clarkson); 35 Steven Wooster (design Clarkson); 36-37 Andrew Lawson; 38 TL Howard Rice/GPL; C Andrew Lawson; B Steven Wooster (design Clarkson); 39 GPL/Brigitte Thomas; 40 TL Andrew Lawson; 4l Steven Wooster; 42 T & B Howard Rice/C & B; C GPL/Mike Paul; 43 GPL/Mike Paul; 44-45 Steven Wooster; 46-47 GPL C: Brigitte Thomas; TR Jerry Pavia; B Howard Rice; 48 TL Steven Wooster; 49 Andrew Lawson (design Beth Chatto); 50 Steven Wooster (except TL: C & B); 52-3 Steven Wooster; 54-55 Steven Wooster; 56 T GPL/Ron Sutherland; B GPL/ Brigitte Thomas; 57 Steven Wooster; 60 Steven Wooster; 62-3 Ian Sidaway; 64-7 Steven Wooster; 68-7l GPL/Henk Dijkmann; 72-75 Steven Wooster (design: Henk Gerritsen); 76-79 GPL/Clive Nichol; 80-83 Steven Wooster (design: Garrett); 84-87 GPL/Mike Paul (design: Anthony Paul); 88-89 Steven Wooster; 90-113 C & B; 114 Andrew Lawson; 116-121 C & B/Howard Rice; 126-127 Andrew Lawson; 128 C & B/ Howard Rice; 129 TL GPL/Clay Perry; TR C & B/Howard Rice; Andrew Lawson; 130-131 C & B/Howard Rice; 132 C & B/Howard Rice; R Andrew Lawson; 133 L & C Steven Wooster: R C & B/Howard Rice; 134-137 C & B/ Howard Rice; l38 L Andrew Lawson; R C & B/Howard Rice; 139 C & B/Howard Rice